KT-548-274

FRENCH

Phrase Book & Dictionary

HarperCollins*Publishers*

First published 1990
Copyright © HarperCollins Publishers
Reprint 10 9
Printed in Italy by Amadeus SpA, Rome

ISBN 0583 31773-1

Your *Collins Phrase Book & Dictionary* is a handy, quick-reference guide that will help you make the most of your stay abroad. Its clear layout, with direct alphabetical access to the relevant information, will save you valuable time when you need that crucial word or phrase.

There are two main sections in this book:

> •70 practical topics arranged in A-Z order from **ACCIDENTS** to **WINTER SPORTS** via such subjects as **MENUS**, **ROOM SERVICE** and **TAXIS**. Each topic gives you the basic phrases you will need along with clear but simple pronunciation guidelines. In many cases, there's the added bonus of our 'Streetwise' travel tips – practical and often invaluable travel information.

> And, if you've found the right phrase but still need a vital word, you're sure to find it in the final topic, **WORDS**, a brief but rigorously practical list of English words and their translations, chosen for their relevance to the needs of the general traveller.

> •A 4000-word foreign vocabulary; the key to all those mystifying but important notices, traffic signs, menus, etc which confront the traveller at every turn. This mini-dictionary will help you enjoy to the full the country's cuisine, save you time when asking directions, and perhaps prevent you getting into one or two tricky situations!

So, just flick through the pages to find the information you require. Why not start with a quick look at the **GRAMMAR**, **ALPHABET** and **PRONUNCIATION** topics? From there on the going is easy with your *Collins Phrase Book & Dictionary*.

Bon voyage!

LIST OF TOPICS

Streetwise

Third party insurance is obligatory. It is best to carry an international Green Card which you can obtain from your insurers. In the case of a traffic offence while under the influence of alcohol, French Police have the power to suspend your driving licence on the spot. If you have an accident, you can choose either to write a mutually agreed statement for insurance purposes or to ask for the police.

There's been an accident	**Il y a eu un accident** *eel ya oo uññ aksee-doñ*
I've crashed my car	**J'ai eu un accident avec ma voiture** *zhay oo uññ aksee-doñ avek ma vwatoor*
Can I see your insurance certificate, please?	**Est-ce que je peux voir votre carte d'assurance?** *es kuh zhuh puh vwahr votr kart dasoo-roñs*
We will have to report it to the police	**Il faut avertir la police** *eel foh avehr-teer la polees*
We should call the police	**Il faudrait appeler la police** *eel fohdreh aplay la polees*
He ran into me	**Il m'est rentré dedans** *eel meh roñtray duhdoñ*
The brakes failed	**Les freins ont lâché** *lay frañ oñ lashay*
He was driving too fast	**Il conduisait trop vite** *eel koñdwee-zeh troh veet*
He did not give way	**Il n'a pas laissé la priorité** *eel na pa lessay la preeo-reetay*

Streetwise

There has been an accident	**Il y a eu un accident** *eel ya oo uñn aksee-doñ*
Call an ambulance/ a doctor	**Appelez une ambulance/un médecin** *aplay oon oñboo-loñs/uñ maydsañ*
He has hurt himself	**Il s'est fait mal** *eel seh feh mal*
I am hurt	**Je me suis fait mal** *zhuh muh swee feh mal*
He is seriously injured/bleeding	**Il est sérieusement blessé/Il saigne** *eel eh say-ryuhz-moñ blessay/eel say-nyuh*
He can't breathe/ move	**Il ne peut pas respirer/bouger** *eel nuh puh pa reh-spee-ray/boo-zhay*
I can't move my arm/leg	**Je ne peux pas bouger le bras/la jambe** *zhuh nuh puh pa boo-zhay luh brah/la zhoñb*
Cover him up	**Couvrez-le** *koovray-luh*
Don't move him	**Ne le bougez pas** *nuh luh boo-zhay pa*
He has broken his arm/cut himself	**Il s'est cassé le bras/s'est coupé** *eel seh kassay luh brah/seh koopay*

See also **EMERGENCIES**

Streetwise

Hotels are officially graded from one to five stars. Prices usually include VAT (TVA) but not breakfast.

We're looking for a hotel/an apartment	**Nous cherchons un hôtel/un appartement** *noo shehrshoñ uñn ohtel/uñn apart-moñ*
I want to reserve a single/double room	**Je voudrais réserver une chambre pour une personne/deux personnes** *zhuh voodray rayzehr-vay oon shoñbr poor oon pehr-son/duh pehr-son*
Is there a restaurant/bar?	**Est-ce qu'il y a un restaurant/bar?** *es keel ya uñ resto-roñ/uñ bar*
Do you have facilities for the disabled?	**Est-ce qu'il y a des aménagements prévus pour les handicapés?** *es keel ya dayz amay-nazh-moñ prayvoo poor lay oñdee-kapay*
I want bed and breakfast/full board	**Je voudrais une chambre avec petit déjeuner/avec la pension complète** *zhuh voodray oon shoñbr avek puhtee day-zhuh-nay/avek la poñ-syoñ koñplet*
What is the daily/weekly rate?	**Quels sont vos prix par jour/par semaine?** *kel soñ voh pree par zhoor/par smen*
I want to stay three nights/from ... till ...	**Je désire rester trois nuits/du ... au ...** *zhuh dayzeer restay trwah nwee/doo ... oh ...*
We'll be arriving at ... /very late	**Nous arriverons à ...** (*see* TIME)**/très tard** *nooz areev-roñ a .../treh tar*
Shall I confirm by letter?	**C'est nécessaire de confirmer par lettre?** *say naysay-sehr duh koñfeer-may par letr*

See also **HOTEL DESK, ROOM SERVICE, SELF-CATERING**

AIRPORT

Where do I check in for the flight to Milan?
Où est-ce que je dois me présenter pour le vol en partance pour Milan?
oo es kuh zhuh dwah muh prayzoñ-tay poor luh vol oñ partoñs poor meeloñ

I'd like an aisle/ a window seat
Je voudrais une place couloir/fenêtre
zhuh voodray oon plas koolwahr/fuhnetr

Will a meal be served on the plane?
Est-ce qu'on nous sert un repas à bord?
es koñ noo sehr uñ ruhpa a bor

Where is the snack bar/duty-free shop?
Où est le snack/la boutique hors-taxe?
oo eh luh snak/la booteek or-tax

Where can I change some money?
Où est-ce que je peux changer de l'argent?
oo es kuh zhuh puh shoñ-zhay duh lar-zhoñ

Where do I get the bus to town?
Où est-ce que je prends le bus pour aller en ville?
oo es kuh zhuh proñ luh boos poor alay oñ veel

Where are the taxis/ telephones?
Où sont les taxis/téléphones?
oo soñ lay taksee/taylay-fon

I want to hire a car/ reserve a hotel room
Je voudrais louer une voiture/réserver une chambre
zhuh voodray loo-ay oon vwatoor/rayzehr-vay oon shoñbr

I am being met
Quelqu'un vient me chercher
kelkuñ vyañ muh shehrshay

The French alphabet is the same as the English one. The pronunciation of each letter is given below it in the following table, together with the word used conventionally for clarification when spelling something out.

A *a*	**comme** *kom*	**Anatole** *ana-tol*		**N** *en*	**comme** *kom*	**Nicolas** *neekoh-la*	
B *bay*	**for**	**Berthe** *behrt*		**O** *oh*	**for**	**Oscar** *oskar*	
C *say*		**Célestin** *sayles-tañ*		**P** *pay*		**Pierre** *pyehr*	
D *day*		**Désiré** *dayzee-ray*		**Q** *koo*		**Quintal** *kañtal*	
E *uh*		**Eugène** *uh-zhen*		**R** *ehr*		**Raoul** *ra-ool*	
F *ef*		**François** *froñswah*		**S** *es*		**Suzanne** *soozan*	
G *zhay*		**Gaston** *gastoñ*		**T** *tay*		**Thérèse** *tayrez*	
H *ash*		**Henri** *oñree*		**U** *oo*		**Ursule** *orrsool*	
I *ee*		**Irma** *eerma*		**V** *vay*		**Viktor** *veektor*	
J *zhee*		**Joseph** *zhohzef*		**W** *doo-bluh-vay*		**William** *weel-yam*	
K *ka*		**Kléber** *klaybehr*		**X** *eex*		**Xavier** *za-vyay*	
L *el*		**Louis** *loo-ee*		**Y** *ee grek*		**Yvonne** *eevon*	
M *em*		**Marcel** *marsel*		**Z** *zed*		**Zoé** *zoh-ay*	

Streetwise

When addressing someone you are not on familiar terms with you should always use the pronoun vous *and the second person plural part of the verb.* Monsieur, Madame *and* Mademoiselle *are used more often than their English equivalents.*

Is it far/expensive?

Est-ce que c'est loin/cher?
es kuh say lwañ/shehr

Do you understand?

Est-ce que vous comprenez?
es kuh voo koñpruh-nay

Can you help me?

Est-ce que vous pouvez m'aider?
es kuh voo poovay meday

Where is the chemist's?

Où est la pharmacie?
oo eh la farma-see

When will it be ready?

Ça sera prêt quand?
sa suhra preh koñ

How do I get there?

Je peux y aller comment?
zhuh puh ee alay komoñ

How far is it to ...?

A quelle distance est ...?
a kel deestoñs eh ...

Is there a good restaurant?

Est-ce qu'il y a un bon restaurant?
es keel ya uñ boñ resto-roñ

What is this?

Qu'est-ce que c'est, ça?
kes kuh say sa

How much is it?

C'est combien?
say koñ-byañ

See also **CONVERSATION**

Most of the beaches in France are open to the public and can be used free of charge. They are usually watched over by lifeguards, especially during the tourist season. The following flags indicate bathing conditions: red = no bathing; orange = bathing is unsafe, but lifeguards are present; green = safe to bathe. Topless sunbathing is permitted on all beaches and some areas are reserved for nudists.

Is it safe to swim here?	**Est-ce qu'on peut se baigner ici sans danger?** *es koñ puh suh bay-nyay eesee soñ doñ-zhay*
When is high/low tide?	**La mer est haute/basse quand?** *la mehr eh oht/bas koñ*
How deep is the water?	**Quelle est la profondeur de l'eau?** *kel eh la profoñ-duhr duh loh*
Are there strong currents?	**Est-ce qu'il y a de forts courants?** *es keel ya duh for kooroñ*
Is it a private/quiet beach?	**Est-ce que c'est une plage privée/tranquille?** *es kuh say oon plazh preevay/troñkeel*
Where do we change?	**Où est-ce qu'on se change?** *oo es koñ suh shoñzh*
Is it possible to hire a deck chair/boat?	**Est-ce qu'il est possible de louer une chaise longue/un bateau?** *es keel eh po-seebl duh loo-ay oon shez loñg/uñ batoh*
Can I go fishing/windsurfing?	**Est-ce que je peux aller à la pêche/faire de la planche à voile?** *es kuh zhuh puh alay a la pesh/fehr duh la ploñsh a vwahl*

See also **WATERSPORTS**

BREAKDOWNS

Streetwise

There are emergency telephones on all motorways and main roads. These provide direct lines to the police. They will come to your aid and put you in touch with a local garage if any repairs are necessary. Repairs can prove expensive so make sure you are properly insured.

My car has broken down	**Ma voiture est en panne** *ma vwatoor eh oñ pan*
There is something wrong with the brakes	**Il y a un problème de freins** *eel ya uñ problem duh frañ*
I have run out of petrol	**Je suis en panne d'essence** *zhuh swee oñ pan dessoñs*
There is a leak in the petrol tank/in the radiator	**Il y a une fuite dans le réservoir d'essence/dans le radiateur** *eel ya oon fweet doñ luh rayzehr-vwahr dessoñs/doñ luh radya-tur*
The windscreen has shattered	**Le parebrise est cassé** *luh parbreez eh kassay*
The engine is overheating	**Le moteur chauffe** *luh motur shohf*
Can you tow me to a garage?	**Pouvez-vous me remorquer jusqu'à un garage?** *poovay-voo muh ruhmor-kay zhooska uñ garazh*
Can you send a mechanic/a breakdown van?	**Est-ce que vous pouvez envoyer un mécanicien/une dépanneuse?** *es kuh voo poovay oñvwah-yay uñ mayka-nee-syañ/oon daypa-nuz*

Office hours vary, but most offices will be open 0900-1200 and 1400-1700, Monday to Friday.

I have an appointment with Mr. Dubois	**J'ai un rendez-vous avec Monsieur Dubois** *zhay uñ roñday-voo avek ...*
He is expecting me	**Il m'attend** *eel matoñ*
Can I leave a message with his secretary?	**Est-ce que je peux laisser un message à sa secrétaire?** *es kuh zhuh puh lessay uñ messazh a sa suhkray-tehr*
I am free tomorrow morning	**Je suis libre demain matin** *zhuh swee leebr duhmañ matañ*
Here is my business card	**Voici ma carte (de visite)** *vwahsee ma kart (duh veezeet)*
Can I send a telex from here?	**Est-ce que je peux envoyer un télex d'ici?** *es kuh zhuh puh oñvwah-yay uñ tayleks deesee*
Where can I get some photocopying done?	**Où est-ce que je pourrais faire faire des photocopies?** *oo es kuh zhuh pooray fehr fehr day foto-kopee*
I want to send this by courier	**Je voudrais envoyer cela par service de messagerie** *zhuh voodray oñvwah-yay suhla par sehrvees duh messa-zhree*
Have you a catalogue/some literature?	**Est-ce que vous avez un catalogue/des brochures?** *es kuh vooz avay uñ kata-log/day broshoor*

Streetwise

Unless you are at the market, where there are precise regulations, be wary of street vendors.

Do you sell postcards/milk?	**Est-ce que vous vendez des cartes postales/du lait?** *es kuh voo voñday day kart pos-tal/doo lay*
How much is that?	**Ça coûte combien?** *sa koot koñ-byañ*
Have you anything smaller/bigger?	**Est-ce que vous avez quelque chose de plus petit/de plus grand?** *es kuh vooz avay kelkuh shohz duh ploo puhtee/duh ploo groñ*
Have you got any bread/matches?	**Est-ce que vous avez du pain/des allumettes?** *es kuh vooz avay doo pañ/dayz aloo-met*
I'd like a newspaper/ some apples	**Je voudrais un journal/des pommes** *zhuh voodray uñ zhoornal/day pom*
A packet of cigarettes, please	**Un paquet de cigarettes, s'il vous plaît** *uñ pakay duh seega-ret seel voo pleh*
I'd like to see the one in the window	**Je voudrais voir celui qui est en vitrine** *zhuh voodray vwahr suh-lwee kee eh oñ veetreen*
I'll take this one/that one there	**Je prends celui-ci/celui-là** *zhuh proñ suh-lwee-see/suh-lwee-la*
Could you wrap it up for me?	**Est-ce que vous pouvez me l'envelopper?** *es kuh voo poovay muh loñ-vlopay*

See also **PAYING, SHOPPING**

Streetwise

There are numerous official camping sites graded with stars according to the facilities they offer. Most of them have a shop on the site. You must not camp without permission in fields or on common land, as penalties are severe. The local tourist office (syndicat d'initiative) will provide details of the facilities in its area.

We are looking for a campsite	**Nous cherchons un camping** *noo shehrshoñ uñ koñping*
Do you have any vacancies?	**Est-ce que vous avez encore de la place?** *es kuh vooz avay oñkor duh la plas*
How much is it per night?	**C'est combien pour une nuit?** *say koñ-byañ poor oon nwee*
We want to stay one night/week	**Nous désirons rester une nuit/semaine** *noo dayzee-roñ restay oon nwee/smen*
May we camp here?	**Est-ce que nous pouvons camper ici?** *es kuh noo poovoñ koñpay eesee*
Can we park our caravan here?	**Pouvons-nous garer notre caravane ici?** *poovoñ-noo garay notr kara-van eesee*
Is there a shop/ restaurant on the site?	**Est-ce qu'il y a une boutique/un restaurant dans le camping?** *es keel ya oon booteek/uñ resto-roñ doñ luh koñping*
Where is the washroom/drinking water?	**Où se trouvent les toilettes?/Où se trouve le robinet d'eau potable?** *oo suh troov lay twalet/oo suh troov luh robee-neh doh pota-bl*

CAR HIRE

Streetwise

Cars can be hired in most towns and at airports and main railway stations. You must be over 20 and have held a full licence for at least a year. Prices normally include maintenance, breakdown service and basic insurance while petrol and any additional insurance are extra. Make sure you know on what basis you will be charged.

I want to hire a car	**Je voudrais louer une voiture** *zhuh voodray loo-ay oon vwatoor*
I need a car with a chauffeur	**J'ai besoin d'une voiture avec chauffeur** *zhay buhzwañ doon vwatoor avek shohfur*
I want a large/small car	**Je voudrais une grande/petite voiture** *zhuh voodray oon groñd/puhteet vwatoor*
Is there a charge per kilometre?	**Est-ce que le kilométrage est en plus?** *es kuh luh keeloh-maytrazh eh oñ ploos*
How much extra is the comprehensive insurance cover?	**Il y a un supplément de combien pour l'assurance tous-risques?** *eel ya uñ sooplay-moñ duh koñ-byañ poor lasoo-roñs too-reesk*
I would like to leave the car in Paris	**Je voudrais laisser la voiture à Paris** *zhuh voodray lessay la vwatoor a paree*
My husband/My wife will be driving as well	**Mon mari/Ma femme conduira aussi** *moñ maree/ma fam koñdwee-ra ohsee*
Is there a radio?	**Est-ce qu'il y a une auto-radio?** *es keel ya oon ohtoh-radyo*
How do I operate the controls?	**Comment fonctionnent les commandes?** *komoñ foñksyon lay komoñd*

Streetwise

French chemists operate a rota system, so that at least one chemist's (pharmacie - *farmasee*) stays open outside normal shop hours. Details are displayed at every chemist's under the heading pharmacie de garde. You will have to pay for all medicines, and you may even have to pay extra at night-time. Your insurance company will advise you about possible reimbursement.

I want something for a headache/a sore throat
Je voudrais quelque chose pour le mal de tête/le mal de gorge
zhuh voodray kelkuh shohz poor luh mal duh tet/luh mal duh gorzh

I would like some aspirin/sticking plaster
Je voudrais de l'aspirine/du sparadrap
zhuh voodray duh laspee-reen/doo spara-dra

Have you anything for sunburn/insect bites/diarrhoea?
Je voudrais quelque chose pour les coups de soleil/les piqûres d'insectes/la diarrhée
zhuh voodray kelkuh shohz poor lay koo duh solay/lay peekoor dañsekt/la dya-ray

I have a cold/I have a cough
Je suis enrhumé/Je tousse
zhuh swee oñroo-may/zhuh tooss

Is this suitable for hay fever/an upset stomach?
C'est bon pour le rhume des foins/un dérangement gastrique?
say boñ poor luh room day fwañ/uñ dayroñzh-moñ gastreek

How much/How many do I take?
J'en prends combien?
zhoñ proñ koñ-byañ

How often do I take it?
J'en prends tous les combien?
zhoñ proñ too lay koñ-byañ

Is it safe for children?
C'est sans danger pour les enfants?
say soñ doñ-zhay poor layz oñfoñ

CHILDREN

Streetwise

Children are normally well catered for in France and they are welcome in bars, restaurants and hotels. Some establishments offer a special menu and they may even have play areas for children. There are many reductions available on transport, in hotels and at museums, cinemas, theatres, etc – the local tourist office will give you details.

I have a small baby/ two children
J'ai un petit bébé/deux enfants
zhay uñ puhtee baybay/duhz oñfoñ

Do you have a special rate for children?
Y a-t-il une réduction pour les enfants?
ee ateel oon raydook-syoñ poor layz onfoñ

What facilities do you have for children?
Qu'est-ce qui est prévu pour les enfants?
kes kee eh prayvoo poor layz onfoñ

Have you got a cot for the baby?
Avez-vous un petit lit pour le bébé?
avay-voo uñ puhtee lee poor luh baybay

Where can I feed/ change the baby?
Où est-ce que je peux allaiter/changer le bébé?
oo es kuh zhuh puh alay-tay/shoñzhay luh baybay

Where can I warm the baby's bottle?
Où est-ce que je peux faire chauffer le biberon du bébé?
oo es kuh zhuh puh fehr shohfay luh beebuh-roñ doo baybay

Is there a playroom?
Est-ce qu'il y a une salle de jeux?
es keel ya oon sal duh zhuh

Is there a babysitting service?
Est-ce qu'il y a un service de babysitting?
es keel ya uñ sehrvees duh baybee-seeting

Streetwise

Visitors to churches should always be suitably dressed, even if they are only there as tourists. Shorts, short skirts and naked shoulders are considered disrespectful and visitors so attired could even find themselves being asked to leave.

Where is the nearest church?	**Où est l'église la plus proche?** *oo eh laygleez la ploo prosh*
Where is there a Protestant church?	**Où est-ce qu'il y a une église protestante?** *oo es keel ya oon aygleez protes-toñt*
I want to see a priest	**Je voudrais voir un prêtre** *zhuh voodray vwahr uñ pretr*
What time is the service?	**A quelle heure est le service (religieux)?** *a kel ur eh luh sehrvees (ruhlee-zhee-uh)*
I want to go to confession	**Je voudrais aller me confesser** *zhuh voodray alay muh koñ-fessay*

CITY TRAVEL

Streetwise

Books of bus tickets can be bought at some tobacconists' and newsagents'. This normally works out cheaper than buying individual tickets. The local tourist board will advise you on the prices of travel passes, which are available in many towns. Once on a bus you should stamp your ticket in the machine provided – only then is it valid. Similarly you should stamp your train ticket in one of the machines on the station platform before you get on the train.

Does this bus/train go to ...?	**Est-ce que ce bus/train va à ...?** *es kuh suh boos/trañ va a ...*
Which bus do I take for the museum?	**Quel bus va au musée?** *kel boos va oh moozay*
Where do I change/ get off?	**Où est-ce que je change/descends?** *oo es kuh zhuh shoñzh/dessoñ*
How frequent are the buses/trains to the city centre?	**Il y a des bus/trains pour le centre-ville tous les combien?** *eel ya day boos/trañ poor luh soñtr-veel too lay koñ-byañ*
Where is the nearest underground station?	**Où est la station de métro la plus proche?** *oo eh la sta-syoñ duh maytroh la ploo prosh*
What is the fare to the town centre?	**Ça coûte combien pour aller au centre-ville?** *sa koot koñ-byañ poor alay oh soñtr-veel*
Where do I buy a ticket?	**Où est-ce qu'on achète un ticket?** *oo es koñ a-shet uñ teekay*
What time is the last bus?	**À quelle heure est le dernier bus?** *a kel ur eh luh dehr-nyay boos*

A dry-cleaner's (une teinturerie - *tañtoo-ruhree* - or un pressing - *presseeng*) is sometimes combined with a laundry (une blanchisserie - *bloñshees-ree*). A launderette is une laverie automatique - *lavree ohtohma-teek*. These are common in France and are cheap and practical. Dry-cleaners' are usually closed on Mondays.

Is there a laundry service?	**Y a-t-il un service de blanchisserie?** *ee ateel uñ sehrvees duh bloñshees-ree*
Is there a launderette/dry-cleaner's nearby?	**Est-ce qu'il y a une laverie automatique/un pressing près d'ici?** *es keel ya oon lavree ohtohma-teek/uñ presseeng preh deesee*
Where can I get this skirt cleaned/ironed?	**Où est-ce que je peux faire nettoyer/faire repasser cette jupe?** *oo es kuh zhuh puh fehr netwa-yay/fehr ruh-passay set zhoop*
Where can I do some washing?	**Où est-ce que je peux faire un peu de lessive?** *oo es kuh zhuh puh fehr uñ puh duh lesseev*
I need some soap and water	**J'ai besoin de savon et d'un peu d'eau** *zhay buhzwañ duh savoñ ay duñ puh doh*
Can you remove this stain?	**Est-ce que vous pouvez faire partir cette tache?** *es kuh voo poovay fehr parteer set tash*
This fabric is very delicate	**C'est un tissu très délicat** *set uñ teesoo treh daylee-ka*
When will my things be ready?	**Mes affaires seront prêtes quand?** *mayz afehr suhroñ pret koñ*

CLOTHES

While continental sizes are used in France, the equivalent British size normally appears on the label.

I take a continental size 40	**Je prends du 40** *zhuh proñ doo karoñt*
Can you measure me?	**Est-ce que vous pouvez prendre mes mesures?** *es kuh voo poovay proñdr may muhzoor*
May I try on this dress?	**Est-ce que je peux essayer cette robe?** *es kuh zhuh puh essay-yay set rob*
May I take it over to the light?	**Est-ce que je peux la voir à la lumière?** *es kuh zhuh puh la vwahr a la loo-myehr*
Where are the changing rooms?	**Où sont les cabines d'essayage?** *oo soñ lay kabeen dessay-yazh*
Is there a mirror?	**Est-ce que vous avez une glace?** *es kuh vooz avay oon glas*
It's too big/small	**C'est trop grand/petit** *say troh groñ/puhtee*
What is the material?	**C'est fait en quoi?** *say feh oñ kwa*
Is it washable?	**Est-ce que c'est lavable?** *es kuh say lava-bl*
I don't like it/I don't like them	**Je ne l'aime pas/Je ne les aime pas** *zhuh nuh lem pa/zhuh nuh layz em pa*
I don't like the colour	**Je n'aime pas la couleur** *zhuh nem pa la koo-lur*

Streetwise

Is there a bus to ...?	**Est-ce qu'il y a un bus pour ...?** *es keel ya uñ boos poor ...*
Which bus goes to ...?	**Quel bus va à ...?** *kel boos va a ...*
Where do I catch the bus for ...?	**Où est-ce que je prends le bus pour ...?** *oo es kuh zhuh proñ luh boos poor ...*
What are the times of the buses to ...?	**Quel est l'horaire des bus pour ...?** *kel eh lorehr day boos poor ...*
Does this bus go to ...?	**Est-ce que ce bus va à ...?** *es kuh suh boos va a ...*
Where do I get off?	**Où est-ce que je descends?** *oo es kuh zhuh dessoñ*
Is there a toilet on board?	**Est-ce qu'il y a des toilettes à bord?** *es keel ya day twalet a bor*
What time does it leave/arrive?	**Il part/Il arrive à quelle heure?** *eel par/eel areev a kel ur*
Will you tell me where to get off?	**Est-ce que vous pouvez me dire quand je dois descendre?** *es kuh voo poovay muh deer koñ zhuh dwah dessoñdr*
Let me off here, please	**Je voudrais descendre ici, s'il vous plaît** *zhuh voodray dessoñdr eesee seel voo pleh*

This does not work	**Ça ne marche pas** *sa nuh marsh pa*
I can't turn the heating off/on	**Je ne peux pas fermer/ouvrir le chauffage** *zhuh nuh puh pa fehrmay/oovreer luh shohfazh*
The lock is broken	**La serrure est cassée** *la sehroor eh kassay*
I can't open the window	**Je ne peux pas ouvrir la fenêtre** *zhuh nuh puh pa oovreer la fuhnetr*
The toilet won't flush	**La chasse d'eau ne marche pas** *la shas doh nuh marsh pa*
There is no hot water/toilet paper	**Il n'y a pas d'eau chaude/de papier hygiénique** *eel nya pa doh shohd/duh papyay ee-zhyay-neek*
The washbasin is dirty	**Le lavabo est sale** *luh lava-boh eh sal*
The room is noisy	**La chambre est bruyante** *la shoñbr eh brwee-yoñt*
My coffee is cold	**Mon café est froid** *moñ kafay eh frwa*
We are still waiting to be served	**On ne nous a pas encore servis** *oñ nuh nooz a pa oñkor sehrvee*
I bought this here yesterday	**J'ai acheté ça ici hier** *zhay ashtay sa eesee yehr*
It has a flaw/hole in it	**Il y a un défaut/un trou** *eel ya uñ dayfoh/uñ troo*

Streetwise

French people shake hands or kiss every time they meet or leave each other. Young people – including good male friends – usually kiss.

Hello/Goodbye	**Bonjour/Au revoir** *boñ-zhoor/oh ruhvwahr*
How do you do?	**Comment allez-vous?** *komoñ talay voo*
Do you speak English?	**Est-ce que vous parlez anglais?** *es kuh voo parlay oñgleh*
I don't speak French	**Je ne parle pas français** *zhuh nuh parl pa froñseh*
What's your name?	**Quel est votre nom?** *kel eh votr noñ*
My name is ...	**Je m'appelle ...** *zhuh mapel*
Do you mind if I sit here?	**Ça vous dérange si je m'assieds ici?** *sa voo dayroñzh see zhuh ma-syay eesee*
I'm English/Scottish/Welsh/Irish/American	**Je suis anglais/écossais/gallois/irlandais/américain** *zhuh swee oñgleh/ayko-seh/galwah/eerloñ-deh/amay-reekañ*
Are you French?	**Est-ce que vous êtes français?** *es kuh vooz et froñseh*
Would you like to come out with me?	**Est-ce que vous voulez sortir avec moi?** *es kuh voo voolay sorteer avek mwah*

CONVERSATION 2

Yes, I should like to	**Oui, avec plaisir** *wee avek playzeer*
Yes please/No thank you	**Oui merci/Non merci** *wee mehrsee/noñ mehrsee*
Thank you (very much)	**Merci (beaucoup)** *mehrsee (bohkoo)*
I'm sorry	**Pardon** *pardoñ*
I'm on holiday here	**Je suis en vacances ici** *zhuh swee oñ vakoñs eesee*
This is my first trip to Paris	**C'est la première fois que je viens à Paris** *say la pruh-myehr fwa kuh zhuh vyañ a paree*
Would you like a drink?	**Est-ce que je peux vous offrir quelque chose à boire?** *es kuh zhuh puh vooz ofreer kelkuh shohz a bwahr*
Have you ever been to Britain?	**Est-ce que vous êtes déjà allé en Grande-Bretagne?** *es kuh vooz et day-zha alay oñ groñd-bruhta-nyuh*
Did you like it there?	**Est-ce que ça vous a plu?** *es kuh sa vooz a ploo*
What part of France are you from?	**D'où est-ce que vous venez en France?** *doo es kuh voo vuhnay oñ froñs*
Can you give me your address?	**Est-ce que vous pouvez me donner votre adresse?** *es kuh voo poovay muh donay votr a-dress*

CONVERSION CHARTS

In the weight and length charts the middle figure can be either metric or imperial. Thus 3.3 feet = 1 metre, 1 foot = 0.3 metres, and so on.

feet		metres	inches		cm	lbs		kg
3.3	1	0.3	0.39	1	2.54	2.2	1	0.45
6.6	2	0.61	0.79	2	5.08	4.4	2	0.91
9.9	3	0.91	1.18	3	7.62	6.6	3	1.4
13.1	4	1.22	1.57	4	10.6	8.8	4	1.8
16.4	5	1.52	1.97	5	12.7	11	5	2.2
19.7	6	1.83	2.36	6	15.2	13.2	6	2.7
23	7	2.13	2.76	7	17.8	15.4	7	3.2
26.2	8	2.44	3.15	8	20.3	17.6	8	3.6
29.5	9	2.74	3.54	9	22.9	19.8	9	4.1
32.9	10	3.05	3.9	10	25.4	22	10	4.5
			4.3	11	27.9			
			4.7	12	30.1			

°C	0	5	10	15	17	20	22	24	26	28	30	35	37	38	40	50	100
°F	32	41	50	59	63	68	72	75	79	82	86	95	98.4	100	104	122	212

Km	10	20	30	40	50	60	70	80	90	100	110	120
Miles	6.2	12.4	18.6	24.9	31	37.3	43.5	49.7	56	62	68.3	74.6

Tyre pressures

lb/sq in	15	18	20	22	24	26	28	30	33	35
kg/sq cm	1.1	1.3	1.4	1.5	1.7	1.8	2	2.1	2.3	2.5

Liquids

gallons	1.1	2.2	3.3	4.4	5.5
litres	5	10	15	20	25

pints	0.44	0.88	1.76
litres	0.25	0.5	1

CUSTOMS & PASSPORTS

I have nothing to
declare

Je n'ai rien à déclarer
zhuh nay ryañ a daykla-ray

I have the usual
allowances of
alcohol/tobacco

**Je n'ai plus que la quantité d'alcool/de
tabac tolerée**
*zhuh nay ploo kuh la koñtee-tay dalkol/duh taba
tolay-ray*

I have two bottles
of wine/a bottle of
spirits to declare

**J'ai deux bouteilles de vin/une bouteille
d'alcool à déclarer**
*zhay duh bootay duh vañ/oon bootay dalkol a
daykla-ray*

My wife/My husband
and I have a joint
passport

**Ma femme/Mon mari et moi sommes sur
le même passeport**
*ma fam/moñ maree ay mwah som soor luh mem
paspor*

The children are
on this passport

Les enfants sont sur ce passeport
layz oñfoñ soñ soor suh paspor

I am a British
national

Je suis de nationalité britannique
zhuh swee duh na-syo-nalee-tay breetaneek

I shall be staying in
France for three
weeks

Je reste trois semaines en France
zhuh rest trwah smen oñ froñs

We are here on
holiday

Nous sommes ici en vacances
noo som eesee oñ vakoñs

I am here on
business

Je suis ici en voyage d'affaires
zhuh swee eesee oñ vwah-yazh dafehr

I have an entry
visa

J'ai un visa
zhay uñ veeza

What is the date today?	**Quelle est la date aujourd'hui?**	*kel eh la dat oh-zhoordwee*
It's the ...	**C'est le ...**	*seh luh ...*
1st of March	**premier mars**	*pruh-myay mars*
2nd of June	**deux juin**	*duh zhwañ*
We will arrive on the 29th of August	**Nous arriverons le vingt-neuf août**	*nooz aree-vuhroñ luh vañt-nuhf oot*
1984	**dix-neuf cent quatre-vingt-quatre**	*deez-nuf-soñ katr-vañ-katr*
Monday	**lundi**	*luñdee*
Tuesday	**mardi**	*mardee*
Wednesday	**mercredi**	*mehrkruh-dee*
Thursday	**jeudi**	*zhuhdee*
Friday	**vendredi**	*voñdruh-dee*
Saturday	**samedi**	*samdee*
Sunday	**dimanche**	*deemoñsh*
January	**janvier**	*zhoñvee-ay*
February	**février**	*fayvree-ay*
March	**mars**	*mars*
April	**avril**	*avreel*
May	**mai**	*may*
June	**juin**	*zhwañ*
July	**juillet**	*zhwee-yeh*
August	**août**	*oot*
September	**septembre**	*septoñbr*
October	**octobre**	*oktobr*
November	**novembre**	*novoñbr*
December	**décembre**	*daysoñbr*

See also **NUMBERS**

DENTIST

Streetwise

Dental treatment is very expensive in France though standards are high. Emergency dentists are listed in local newspapers. They provide a 24-hour service but will charge a high price and will expect to be paid on the spot.

I need to see the dentist (urgently)	**Je dois voir le dentiste (d'urgence)** *zhuh dwah vwahr luh doñteest (door-zhoñs)*
I have toothache	**J'ai mal aux dents** *zhay mal oh doñ*
I've broken a tooth	**J'ai une dent de cassée** *zhay oon doñ duh kassay*
A filling has come out	**Un plombage est parti** *uñ ploñbazh eh partee*
My gums are bleeding/ are sore	**Mes gencives saignent/me font mal** *may zhoñseev say-nyuh/muh foñ mal*
Please give me an injection	**Vous voulez bien me faire une piqûre** *voo voolay byañ muh fehr oon peekoor*
My dentures need repairing	**C'est nécessaire de réparer mon dentier** *say naysay-sehr duh raypa-ray moñ doñ-tyay*

THE DENTIST MAY SAY:

Je dois l'enlever
zhuh dwah loñluh-vay

I shall have to take it out

Il faut faire un plombage
eel foh fehr uñ ploñbazh

You need a filling

Ça va peut-être vous faire un peu mal
sa va puht-etr voo fehr uñ puh mal

This might hurt a bit

Where is the nearest post office?	**La poste la plus proche, s'il vous plaît?** *la post la ploo prosh, seel voo pleh*
How do I get to the airport?	**Pour aller à l'aéroport, s'il vous plaît?** *poor alay a la-ehro-por seel voo pleh*
Can you tell me the way to the station?	**Pour aller à la gare, s'il vous plaît?** *poor alay a la gar seel voo pleh*
Is this the right way to the cathedral?	**Est-ce que c'est la direction de la cathédrale?** *es kuh say la deerek-syoñ duh la katay-dral*
I am looking for the tourist information office	**Je cherche le syndicat d'initiative** *zhuh shersh luh sañdee-ka deenee-sya-teev*
Is it far to walk/by car?	**Est-ce que c'est loin à pied/en voiture?** *es kuh say lwañ a pyay/oñ vwatoor*
Which road do I take for ...?	**La route pour aller à ..., s'il vous plaît?** *la root poor alay a ... seel voo pleh*
Is this the turning for ...?	**Est-ce que c'est là que je tourne pour ...?** *es kuh say la kuh zhuh toorn poor ...*
How do I get onto the motorway?	**Pour rejoindre l'autoroute, s'il vous plaît?** *poor ruh-zhwañdruh lohtoh-root seel voo pleh*
Can you show me on the map?	**Est-ce que vous pouvez me montrer sur la carte?** *es kuh voo poovay muh moñtray soor la kart*

DOCTOR

Medical treatment has to be paid for on the spot. While form E111 (which should be obtained before departure) enables British and Irish visitors to reclaim a proportion of costs, proper accident/medical insurance is still advisable. Doctors are private but their fees are regulated by the government.

I need a doctor
J'ai besoin d'un docteur
zhay buhzwañ duñ doktur

Can I make an appointment?
Est-ce que je peux prendre rendez-vous?
es kuh zhuh puh proñdr roñday-voo

My wife is ill
Ma femme est malade
ma fam eh malad

I have a sore throat
J'ai mal à la gorge
zhay mal a la gorzh

He has diarrhoea/ earache
Il a la diarrhée/Il a mal à l'oreille
eel a la dya-ray/eel a mal a loray

I am constipated
Je suis constipé
zhuh swee koñstee-pay

I have a pain here/ in my chest
J'ai mal ici/dans la poitrine
zhay mal eesee/doñ la pwahtreen

He has been stung/ bitten
Il a été piqué/mordu
eel a aytay peekay/mordoo

He can't breathe/ walk
Il a de la difficulté à respirer/marcher
eel a duh la deefee-kooltay a reh-spee-ray/ marshay

I feel dizzy
J'ai la tête qui tourne
zhay la tet kee toorn

I can't sleep/ swallow	**J'ai de la difficulté à dormir/avaler** *zhay duh la deefee-kooltay a dormeer/ava-lay*
She has been sick	**Elle a vomi** *el a vomee*
I am diabetic/ pregnant	**Je suis diabétique/enceinte** *zhuh swee dya-bay-teek/oñsañt*
I am allergic to penicillin/cortisone	**Je suis allergique à la pénicilline/à la cortisone** *zhuh swee alehr-zheek a la paynee-seeleen/a la kortee-zon*
I have high blood pressure	**Je fais de la tension** *zhuh feh duh la toñ-syoñ*
My blood group is A positive/O negative	**Mon groupe sanguin est rhésus A positif/ rhésus O négatif** *moñ groop soñgañ eh rayzoos a pozee-teef/ rayzoos oh nayga-teef*

THE DOCTOR MAY SAY:

Vous devez rester couché
voo duhvay restay kooshay

You must stay in bed

Il faut le transporter à l'hôpital
eel foh luh troñspor-tay a lopee-tal

He will have to go to hospital

Il faut vous opérer
eel foh vooz opay-ray

You will need an operation

Prenez cela trois/quatre fois par jour
pruhnay suhla trwah/katr fwah par zhoor

Take this three/four times a day

See also **ACCIDENTS - INJURIES, DENTIST**

DRINKS

Streetwise

A black/white coffee, please
Un café noir/café crème, s'il vous plaît
uñ kafay nwahr/kafay krem seel voo pleh

Two cups of tea
Deux thés
duh tay

A pot of tea
Un pot de thé
uñ poh duh tay

A glass of lemonade
Un verre de limonade
uñ vehr duh leemo-nad

A bottle of mineral water
Une bouteille d'eau minérale
oon bootay doh meenay-ral

A draught beer
Une bière à la pression
oon bee-ayr a la preh-syoñ

With ice, please
Avec des glaçons, s'il vous plaît
avek day glasoñ seel voo pleh

Do you have ...?
Est-ce que vous avez ...?
es kuh vooz avay ...

Another coffee, please
Encore un café, s'il vous plaît
oñkor uñ kafay seel voo pleh

See also **WINES & SPIRITS**

What is the speed
limit on this road?

Sur cette route, la vitesse est limitée à combien?
soor set root la veetess eh leemee-tay a koñ-byañ

Are seat belts
compulsory?

Est-ce que les ceintures de sécurité sont obligatoires?
es kuh lay sañtoor duh saykoo-reetay soñ oblee-gatwahr

Is there a toll on
this motorway?

Est-ce que c'est une autoroute à péage?
es kuh say oon ohtoh-root a pay-yazh

Is there a short-cut?

Est-ce qu'il y a un raccourci?
es keel ya uñ rakoor-see

Where can I park?

Où est-ce que je peux me garer?
oo es kuh zhuh puh muh garay

Is there a car park
nearby?

Est-ce qu'il y a un parking près d'ici?
es keel ya uñ parkeeng preh deesee

How long can I stay
here?

Je peux rester ici combien de temps?
zhuh puh restay eesee koñ-byañ duh toñ

Do I need a parking
disc?

Est-ce qu'il faut un disque de stationnement?
es keel foh uñ deesk duh sta-syon-moñ

See also ACCIDENTS - CARS, BREAKDOWNS, PETROL STATION, POLICE

EATING OUT

Streetwise

The Les Routiers *sign (symbol of the truck-drivers association)*
indicates that a restaurant serves good basic meals at a reasonable
price. Menus touristiques *in places obviously catering for tourists may*
not always be of the highest standard.

Is there a restaurant/café near here?	**Y a-t-il un restaurant/café près d'ici?** *ee ateel uñ resto-roñ/kafay preh deesee*
A table for four, please	**Une table pour quatre, s'il vous plaît** *oon tabl poor katr seel voo pleh*
May we see the menu?	**Le menu, s'il vous plaît** *luh muhnoo, seel voo pleh*
We'll take the set menu, please	**Nous prendrons le menu, s'il vous plaît** *noo proñdroñ luh muhnoo seel voo pleh*
We'd like a drink first	**Nous commencerons par un apéritif** *noo komoñs-ron par uñn apay-reeteef*
Do you have a menu for children?	**Avez-vous un menu pour les enfants?** *avay-voo uñ muhnoo poor layz oñfoñ*
Could we have some more bread/water?	**Encore du pain/de l'eau, s'il vous plaît** *oñkor du pañ/duh loh seel voo pleh*
We'd like a dessert	**Nous aimerions un dessert** *nooz aym-ryoñ uñ dessehr*
The bill, please	**L'addition, s'il vous plaît** *ladee-syoñ seel voo pleh*
Is service included?	**Est-ce que le service est compris?** *es kuh luh sehrvees eh koñpree*

See also DRINKS, ORDERING, PAYING, TIPPING

Streetwise

There's a fire!
Il y a le feu!
eel ya luh fuh

Call a doctor/an ambulance!
Appelez un docteur/une ambulance!
aplay uñ doktur/oon oñboo-loñs

We must get him to hospital
Il faut le transporter à l'hôpital
eel foh luh troñspor-tay a lopee-tal

Fetch help quickly!
Allez chercher de l'aide, vite!
alay shershay duh led veet

Get the police!
Appelez la police!
aplay la polees

Where's the nearest police station/hospital?
Où est le commissariat/l'hôpital le plus proche?
oo eh luh komee-saree-a/lopee-tal luh ploo prosh

I've lost my credit card/my wallet
J'ai perdu ma carte de crédit/mon portefeuille
zhay pehrdoo ma kart duh kraydee/moñ port-fuhy

My child/My handbag is missing
Mon enfant/Mon sac a disparu
mon oñfoñ/moñ sak a deespa-roo

My passport/My watch has been stolen
On m'a volé mon passeport/ma montre
oñ ma volay moñ paspor/ma moñtr

I've forgotten my ticket/my key
J'ai oublié mon billet/ma clé
zhay ooblee-ay moñ bee-yay/ma klay

See also **ACCIDENTS, BREAKDOWNS, DENTIST, DOCTOR**

Streetwise

Films are usually dubbed and shown without subtitles, except for those advertised as 'VO' ('version originale' - 'in the original language') or 'sous-titrée' ('with subtitles').

Are there any local festivals?	**Est-ce qu'il y a des festivités locales?** *es keel ya day festee-veetay lo-kal*
Can you recommend something for the children?	**Pouvez-vous recommander quelque chose pour les enfants?** *poovay-voo ruhko-moñday kelkuh shohz poor layz oñfoñ*
What is there to do in the evenings?	**Qu'est-ce qu'il y a à faire le soir?** *kes keel ya a fehr luh swahr*
Where is there a cinema/theatre?	**Où est-ce qu'il y a un cinéma/théâtre?** *oo es keel ya uñ seenay-ma/tayatr*
Can you book the tickets for us?	**Pouvez-vous nous réserver les billets?** *poovay-voo noo rayzehr-vay lay bee-yay*
Are there any night clubs?	**Y a-t-il des boîtes de nuit?** *ee ateel day bwaht duh nwee*
Is there a swimming pool?	**Est-ce qu'il y a une piscine?** *es keel ya oon peeseen*
Can we go fishing/ riding?	**Est-ce qu'on peut pêcher/faire du cheval?** *es koñ puh payshay/fehr doo shuhval*
Where can we play tennis/golf?	**Où est-ce qu'on peut faire du tennis/golf?** *oo es koñ puh fehr doo tenees/golf*
Can we hire the equipment?	**Est-ce qu'on peut louer le matériel?** *es koñ puh loo-ay luh matay-ryel*

See also **NIGHTLIFE, SIGHTSEEING**

What time is the next sailing?

La prochaine traversée est à quelle heure?
la proshen travehr-say eh a kel ur

A return ticket for one car, two adults and two children

Un aller-retour pour une voiture, deux adultes et deux enfants
uññ alay-ruhtoor poor oon vwatoor duhz adoolt ay duhz oñfoñ

How long does the crossing take?

La traversée dure combien de temps?
la travehr-say door koñ-byañ duh toñ

Are there any cabins/reclining seats?

Est-ce qu'il y a des cabines/sièges inclinables?
es keel ya day kabeen/syezh añklee-nabl

Is there a TV lounge/a bar?

Est-ce qu'il y a une salle de télé/un bar?
es keel ya oon sal duh taylay/uñ bar

Where are the toilets?

Où sont les toilettes?
oo soñ lay twalet

Where is the duty-free shop?

Où est la boutique hors-taxe?
oo eh la bootek or-tax

Can we go out on deck?

Est-ce qu'on peut sortir sur le pont?
es koñ puh sorteer soor luh poñ

What is the sea like today?

La mer est comment, aujourd'hui?
la mehr eh komoñ oh-zhoordwee

GIFTS & SOUVENIRS

Where can we buy souvenirs of the cathedral?	**Où est-ce qu'on peut acheter des souvenirs de la cathédrale?** *oo es koñ puh ashtay day soov-neer duh la katay-dral*
Where is the nearest gift shop?	**Où est la boutique de souvenirs la plus proche?** *oo eh la booteek duh soov-neer la ploo prosh*
I want to buy a present for my husband/my wife	**Je voudrais acheter un cadeau pour mon mari/ma femme** *zhuh voodray ashtay uñ kadoh poor moñ maree/ma fam*
What is the local speciality?	**Quelle est la spécialité locale?** *kel eh la spay-sya-leetay lo-kal*
Is this hand-made?	**C'est fait main?** *say feh mañ*
I want something cheaper/more expensive	**Je voudrais quelque chose de moins cher/de plus cher** *zhuh voodray kelkuh shohz duh mwañ shehr/ duh ploo shehr*
Will this cheese/ wine travel well?	**Est-ce que ce fromage/vin supporte bien le voyage?** *es kuh suh fromazh/vañ sooport byañ luh vwah-yazh*
Do you have any postcards/a guide book?	**Avez-vous des cartes postales/un guide?** *avay-voo day kart pos-tal/uñ geed*
Please wrap it up for me	**Enveloppez-le-moi, s'il vous plaît** *oñ-vlopay-luh-mwah seel voo pleh*

Nouns

In French, all nouns are either masculine or feminine. Where in
English we say 'the apple' and 'the book', in French it is **la pomme**
and **le livre** because *pomme* is feminine and *livre* is masculine.
The gender of nouns is shown in the 'article' (= words for 'the' and
'a') used before them:

	Words for 'the':	Words for 'a':
masculine	**le, l'** (before a vowel: l'avion)	**un**
feminine	**la, l'** (before a vowel: l'eau)	**une**

To form the plural of most nouns in French, an **-s** is added to the
singular, as in English. But unlike English, the **-s** is not pronounced.
The form 'the' for plural nouns in French, regardless of gender, is **les**,
hence:

> **les livres** (the books)
> *lay leevr*

> **les pommes** (the apples)
> *lay pom*

NOTE: When used after the words **à** (to, at) and **de** (of, from), the words
le and **les** contract as follows:

> **à+le = au** *oh*
> **à+les = aux** *oh*

> **de+le = du** *doo*
> **de+les = des** *day*

e.g. **au cinéma** (to the cinema)
le prix du billet (the price of the ticket)

'This', That', 'These', 'Those'

Again these depend on the gender and number of the noun they
precede:

> **ce livre** (this or that book)
> **cette pomme** (this or that apple)
> **ces livres/pommes** (these or those books/apples)

The distinction between this/these and that/those can be made by
adding **-ci** or **-là** to the noun:

> **ce livre-ci** (this book)

> **ce livre-là** (that book)

GRAMMAR 2

Adjectives

Adjectives normally follow the noun they describe in French, e.g. **la pomme verte** (the green apple). Some common exceptions which precede the noun are:

beau beautiful, **bon** good, **grand** big, **haut** high, **jeune** young, **long** long, **joli** pretty, **mauvais** bad, **nouveau** new, **petit** small, **vieux** old.

French adjectives have to reflect the gender of the noun they describe. To make an adjective feminine, an **-e** is added to the masculine form (where this does not already end in **-e**). The masculine form is the form found in the dictionary. A final consonant usually silent in the masculine form is pronounced in the feminine, thus:

masc.	**le livre vert**	*fem.*	**la pomme verte**
	luh leevr vehr		*la pom vehrt*
	(the green book)		(the green apple)

To make an adjective plural an **-s** is added to the singular form, but not sounded:

masc.	**les livres verts**	*fem.*	**les pommes vertes**
	lay leevr vehr		*lay pom vehrt*
	(the green books)		(the green apples)

'My', 'Your', 'His', 'Her'

These words also depend on the gender and number of the following noun and not on the sex of the 'owner':

	with masc. noun		with fem. noun		with plural nouns	
my	**mon**	*(moñ)*	**ma**	*(ma)*	**mes**	*(may)*
your	**votre**	*(votr)*	**votre**	*(votr)*	**vos**	*(voh)*
his/her*	**son**	*(soñ)*	**sa**	*(sa)*	**ses**	*(say)*

****NOTE:** There is no distinction between 'his' and 'her':

le billet	the ticket
son billet	his/her ticket

Pronouns

SUBJECT			OBJECT		
I	**je, j'** (before vowel)	*zhuh*	me	**me, m'**	*muh*
you	**vous**	*voo*	you	**vous**	*voo*
he/it	**il**	*eel*	him/it	**le, l'**	*luh*
she/it	**elle**	*el*	her/it	**la, l'**	*la*
we	**nous**	*noo*	us	**nous**	*noo*
they *(masc.)*	**ils**	*eel*	them	**les**	*lay*
(fem.)	**elles**	*el*			

NOTES:

1. Object pronouns are placed *before* the verb:

   > **il** (he) **vous** (you) **aime**   he loves you
   > **nous** (we) **la** (her) **connaissons**   we know her

   However, in commands or requests, the pronouns follow the verb, as in English:

   > **écoutez-*le***   listen to him
   > **aidez-*moi*** *   help me

   (But in commands expressed in the negative, e.g. *don't do it*, the pronouns precede the verb: **ne le faites pas** *don't do it*)

2. The object pronouns shown above are used to mean *to me, to us* etc., except:

   > **le** and **la** become **lui** *(lwee)*
   > **les** becomes **leur** *(lur)*:

   e.g.   **il** (he) **le** (it) **lui** (to him) **donne**
         he gives it to him

*This stressed form of **me** is used after the verb.

GRAMMAR 4

Verbs

There are three main patterns of endings for verbs in French – those ending -er, -ir, and -re in the dictionary:

donner	to give	**finir**	to finish
je donne *zhuh don*	I give	**je finis** *zhuh feenee*	I finish
vous donnez *voo donay*	you give	**vous finissez** *voo feenee-say*	you finish
il/elle donne *eel/el don*	he/she gives	**il/elle finit** *eel/el feenee*	he/she finishes
nous donnons *noo donoñ*	we give	**nous finissons** *noo feenee-soñ*	we finish
ils/elles donnent *eel/el don*	they give	**ils/elles finissent** *eel/el feenees*	they finish

répondre	to reply
je réponds *zhuh raypoñ*	I reply
vous répondez *voo raypoñ-day*	you reply
il/elle répond *eel/el raypoñ*	he/she replies
nous répondons *noo raypoñ-doñ*	we reply
ils/elles répondent *eel/el raypoñd*	they reply

And in the past:

j'ai donné I gave *zhay donay*	**j'ai fini** I finished *zhay feenee*	**j'ai répondu** I replied *zhay raypoñ-doo*

For the rest of this tense, see **avoir** below.

Three of the most common verbs are irregular:

être to be

Je suis I am
zhuh swee

vous êtes you are
vooz et

il/elle est he/she is
eel/el eh

nous sommes we are
noo som

ils/elles sont they are
eel/el soñ

avoir to have

j'ai I have
zhay

vous avez you have
vooz avay

il/elle a he/she has
eel/el a

nous avons we have
nooz avoñ

ils/elles ont they have
eelz/elz oñ

aller to go

je vais I go
zhuh vay

vous allez you go
vooz alay

il/elle va he/she goes
eel/el va

nous allons we go
nooz aloñ

ils/elles vont they go
eel/el voñ

GREETINGS

Streetwise

Hello	**Bonjour** *boñ-zhoor*
Good morning/Good afternoon	**Bonjour** *boñ-zhoor*
Good evening	**Bonsoir** *boñswahr*
Goodbye	**Au revoir** *oh ruhvwahr*
Good night	**Bonsoir** *boñswahr*
How do you do?	**Enchanté (de faire votre connaissance)** *oñshoñ-tay (duh fehr votre koneh-soñs)*
Pleased to meet you	**Enchanté** *oñshoñ-tay*
How are you?	**Comment ça va?** *komoñ sa va*
Fine, thank you	**Très bien, merci** *treh byañ mehrsee*

Streetwise

Hairdressers' are normally closed on Mondays.

I'd like to make an appointment	**Je voudrais prendre rendez-vous** *zhuh voodray proñdr roñday-voo*
A cut and blow-dry, please	**Coupe et brushing, s'il vous plaît** *koop ay bruhshing seel voo pleh*
A shampoo and set	**Shampooing et mise en plis** *shoñpwañ ay meez oñ plee*
Not too short	**Pas trop court** *pa troh koor*
I'd like it layered	**Je voudrais une coupe en dégrade** *zhuh voodray oon koop oñ daygra-day*
Not too much off the back/the fringe	**Ne coupez pas trop derrière/la frange** *nuh koopay pa troh deh-ryehr/la froñzh*
Take more off the top/the sides	**Un peu plus court sur le dessus/les côtés** *uñ puh ploo koor soor luh duhsoo/lay kohtay*
My hair is permed/tinted	**J'ai une permanente/une coloration** *zhay oon pehrma-noñt/oon kolo-ra-syoñ*
My hair is naturally curly/straight	**Mes cheveux frisent/sont raides naturellement** *may shuhvuh freez/soñ red natoo-relmoñ*
It's too hot	**C'est trop chaud** *say troh shoh*
I'd like a conditioner, please	**Un baume démêlant, s'il vous plaît** *uñ bom day-meh-yoñ seel voo pleh*

HOTEL DESK

Streetwise

You normally have to be out of your room by 1000 on the day you leave your hotel. A service charge is normally included in your bill but it is still usual to tip the staff.

I reserved a room
in the name of ...

J'ai réservé une chambre au nom de ...
zhay rayzehr-vay oon shoñbr oh noñ duh

I confirmed my
booking by phone/
by letter

**J'ai confirmé ma réservation par
téléphone/lettre**
*zhay koñfeer-may ma rayzehr-va-syoñ par
taylay-fon/letr*

Could you have my
luggage taken up?

Vous pouvez faire monter mes bagages?
voo poovay fehr moñtay may bagazh

What time is
breakfast/dinner?

**Le petit déjeuner/Le dîner est à quelle
heure?**
luh puhtee day-zhuh-nay/luh deenay eh a kel ur

Can we have a
packed lunch for
our picnic?

**Est-ce que nous pouvons avoir un
panier-repas pour notre pique-nique?**
*es kuh noo poovoñ avwahr uñ pa-nyay-ruhpa
poor notr peek-neek*

Please call me at ...

Réveillez-moi à ... (*see* TIME), **s'il vous plaît**
rayvay-yay-mwah a ... seel voo pleh

My key, please

Ma clé, s'il vous plaît
ma klay seel voo pleh

I want to stay an
extra night

Je voudrais rester une nuit supplémentaire
zhuh voodray restay oon nwee sooplay-moñtehr

I shall be leaving
at ... tomorrow
morning

Je partirai demain matin à ... (*see* TIME)
zhuh partee-ray duhmañ matañ a ...

48

See also **ACCOMMODATION, PAYING, ROOM SERVICE**

Streetwise

You will find a left-luggage office (la consigne) in every railway station and airport.

Where do I check in my luggage?	**Où est-ce qu'on enregistre les bagages?** *oo es koñ oñruh-zheestr lay bagazh*
Where is the luggage from the London flight/train?	**Où sont les bagages du vol/train en provenance de Londres?** *oo soñ lay bagazh doo vol/trañ oñ provnoñs duh loñdr*
Our luggage has not arrived	**Nos bagages ne sont pas arrivés** *noh bagazh nuh soñ pa aree-vay*
My suitcase was damaged in transit	**Ma valise a été endommagé pendant le voyage** *ma valeez a aytay oñdo-ma-zhay poñdoñ luh vwah-yazh*
Where is the left-luggage office?	**Où est la consigne?** *oo eh la koñsee-nyuh*
Are there any luggage trolleys?	**Est-ce qu'il y a des chariots à bagages?** *es keel ya day sha-ryoh a bagazh*
Can you help me with my bags please?	**Est-ce que vous pouvez m'aider à porter mes bagages?** *es kuh voo poovay meday a portay may bagazh*
Please take my bags to a taxi	**Est-ce que vous pouvez porter mes bagages jusqu'à un taxi?** *es kuh voo poovay portay may bagazh zhooska uñ taksee*
I sent my luggage on in advance	**J'ai envoyé mes bagages à l'avance** *zhay oñvwah-yay may bagazh a lavoñs*

Streetwise

Maps can be bought at newsagents' but they may also be obtained free from the tourist office.

Where can I buy a local map?	**Où est-ce que je peux acheter une carte de la région?** *oo es kuh zhuh puh ashtay oon kart duh la ray-zhyoñ*
Have you got a town plan?	**Est-ce que vous avez un plan de la ville?** *es kuh vooz avay uñ ploñ duh la veel*
I want a street map of the city	**Je voudrais un plan de la ville** *zhuh voodray uñ ploñ duh la veel*
I need a road map of ...	**J'ai besoin d'une carte routière de ...** *zhay buhzwañ doon kart roo-tyehr duh ...*
Can I get a map at the tourist office?	**Est-ce que je peux obtenir un plan au syndicat d'initiative?** *es kuh zhuh puh optuh-neer uñ ploñ oh sañdee-ka deenee-sya-teev*
Can you show me on the map?	**Est-ce que vous pouvez me montrer sur la carte?** *es kuh voo poovay muh moñtray soor la kart*
Do you have a guidebook in English?	**Est-ce que vous avez un guide touristique en anglais?** *es kuh vooz avay uñ geed toorees-teek oñn oñgleh*
Do you have a guidebook to the cathedral?	**Est-ce que vous avez un guide sur la cathédrale?** *es kuh vooz avay uñ geed soor la katay-dral*

See also **DIRECTIONS**

a pint of ...
un demi-litre de ...
uñ duhmee leetr duh

a litre of ...
un litre de ...
uñ leetr duh

a kilo of ...
un kilo de ...
uñ keeloh duh

a pound of ...
une livre de ...
oon leevr duh

100 grammes of ...
cent grammes de ...
soñ gram duh

half a kilo of ...
une livre de ...
oon leevr duh

a half-bottle of ...
une demi-bouteille de ...
oon duhmee-bootay duh

a slice of ...
une tranche de ...
oon troñsh duh

a portion of ...
une portion de ...
oon por-syoñ duh

a dozen ...
une douzaine de ...
oon doozen duh

150 francs worth of ...
pour 150 francs de ...
poor soñ-sañkoñt froñ duh

a third
un tiers
uñ tyehr

two thirds
deux tiers
duh tyehr

a quarter
un quart
uñ kar

three quarters
trois quarts
trwah kar

ten per cent
dix pour cent
dee poor soñ

more
plus
ploos

less
moins
mwañ

enough
assez
assay

double
le double
luh doobl

twice
deux fois
duh fwah

three times
trois fois
trwah fwah

See also **BUYING, CONVERSIONS CHARTS, NUMBERS, PAYING**

The French eat three main meals per day:

Le petit déjeuner (breakfast) is normally a fairly light meal consisting of little more than a slice of bread and jam or a *croissant.* On Sundays and during the holidays, however, a little more effort goes into the meal and fresh *baguettes, brioches* and *croissants* are consumed. At all times the usual breakfast drink is *café au lait* (white coffee).

Le déjeuner (lunch), eaten as early as mid-day, is traditionally the most important meal of the day, although with fewer people taking a long lunch break, many now take lunch in a restaurant near their place of work. They will often choose from the *menu du jour* (set-price business lunch) which normally represents good value for money. On Sundays and during the holidays lunch remains the main meal of the day.

Le dîner (dinner) is for many the only meal which they take with their family during the week. It is normally taken around 8 pm, although in the east it is often eaten earlier while in the south it may be taken later.

Generally, the courses on a menu will be as follows for both lunch and dinner:

Entrée – starter (normally cold meat or salad)
Potage – soup
Plat de résistance – main course (meat and vegetables)
Fromage – cheese
Dessert – dessert
Café – coffee

What is the dish of the day?	**Quel(le) est le plat du jour?** *kel eh luh pla doo zhoor*
What kind of starters/ vegetables/fruit do you have?	**Qu'est-ce que vous avez comme entrées/ légumes/fruits?** *kes kuh vooz avay kom oñtray/laygoom/frwee*
Can I have some salt/ pepper/mustard?	**Est-ce que je pourrais avoir du sel/du poivre/de la moutarde?** *es kuh zhuh pooray avwahr doo sel/doo pwavr/ duh la mootard*

See also **EATING OUT, ORDERING, WINES & SPIRITS**

*The French currency is the franc, which consists of 100 centimes.
Bureaux de change are to be found in many hotels, railway stations
and airports. These stay open longer than banks.*

I haven't enough
money

Je n'ai pas assez d'argent
zhuh nay pa assay dar-zhoñ

Have you any
change?

Est-ce que vous avez de la monnaie?
es kuh vooz avay duh la monay

Can you change a
50 franc note?

**Est-ce que vous avez la monnaie de 50
francs?**
es kuh vooz avay la monay duh sañkoñt froñ

I'd like to change
these traveller's
cheques

Je voudrais changer ces travellers
zhuh voodray shoñ-zhay say trav-lurz

I want to change
some francs into
pounds

Je voudrais changer des francs en livres
zhuh voodray shoñ-zhay day froñ oñ leevr

What is the rate for
sterling/dollars?

Combien vaut la livre/le dollar?
koñ-byañ voh la leevr/luh dollar

Can I get a cash
advance with my
credit card?

**Est-ce que je peux obtenir de l'argent
liquide avec ma carte de crédit?**
*es kuh zhuh puh optuh-neer duh lar-zhoñ
leekeed avek ma kart duh kraydee*

I should like to
transfer some
money from my
bank in ...

**Je voudrais transférer de l'argent de ma
banque à ...**
*zhuh voodray troñsfay-ray duh lar-zhoñ duh ma
boñk a ...*

NIGHTLIFE

Streetwise

Entrance fees at discos usually include the price of your first drink. An evening out at a café théâtre or café concert, where you can enjoy a drink and listen to live music without paying an entrance fee, can be very entertaining.

What is there to do in the evenings?	**Qu'est-ce qu'on peut faire le soir?** *kes koñ puh fehr luh swahr*
Where can we go to dance/to see a cabaret?	**Où est-ce qu'on peut aller danser/voir un spectacle de cabaret?** *oo es koñ puh alay doñsay/vwahr uñ spekta-kl duh kaba-reh*
Are there any good night clubs/discos?	**Est-ce qu'il y a de bonnes boîtes de nuit/de bonnes discos?** *es keel ya duh bon bwaht duh nwee/duh bon deeskoh*
How much does it cost to get in?	**L'entrée coûte combien?** *loñtray koot koñ-byañ*
We'd like to reserve two seats for tonight	**Nous désirons réserver deux places pour ce soir** *noo dayzee-roñ rayzehr-vay duh plas poor suh swahr*
Is there a bar/a restaurant?	**Est-ce qu'il y a un bar/un restaurant?** *es keel ya uñ bar/uñ resto-rañ*
What time does the show/concert begin?	**Le spectacle/concert commence à quelle heure?** *luh spek-takl/koñsehr komoñs a kel ur*
How long does the performance last?	**Le spectacle dure combien de temps?** *luh spek-takl door koñ-byañ duh toñ*

See also **EATING OUT, ENTERTAINMENT**

0	**zéro** _zayroh_	13	**treize** _trez_	50	**cinquante** _sañkoñt_
1	**un** _uñ_	14	**quatorze** _katorz_	60	**soixante** _swasoñt_
2	**deux** _duh_	15	**quinze** _kañz_	70	**soixante-dix** _swasoñt-dees_
3	**trois** _trwah_	16	**seize** _sez_	80	**quatre-vingts** _katr-vañ_
4	**quatre** _katr_	17	**dix-sept** _dees-set_	90	**quatre-vingt-dix** _katr-vañ-dees_
5	**cinq** _sañk_	18	**dix-huit** _deez-weet_	100	**cent** _soñ_
6	**six** _sees_	19	**dix-neuf** _deez-nuhf_	110	**cent dix** _soñ dees_
7	**sept** _set_	20	**vingt** _vañ_	200	**deux cents** _duh soñ_
8	**huit** _weet_	21	**vingt et un** _vañt ay uñ_	300	**trois cents** _trwah soñ_
9	**neuf** _nuhf_	22	**vingt-deux** _vañ-duh_	1,000	**mille** _meel_
10	**dix** _dees_	23	**vingt-trois** _vañ-trwah_	2,000	**deux mille** _duh meel_
11	**onze** _oñz_	30	**trente** _troñt_	1,000,000	**un million** _uñ mee-lyoñ_
12	**douze** _dooz_	40	**quarante** _karoñt_		

1st	**premier/première** _pruh-myay/pruh-myehr_	5th	**cinquième** _sañ-kyem_	9th	**neuvième** _nuh-vyem_
2nd	**deuxième** _duh-zyem_	6th	**sixième** _see-zyem_	10th	**dixième** _dee-zyem_
3rd	**troisième** _trwah-zyem_	7th	**septième** _seh-tyem_		
4th	**quatrième** _katree-yem_	8th	**huitième** _wee-tyem_		

See also **MEASUREMENTS**

ORDERING

French cuisine is very varied and regional specialities are always worth trying – ask the waiter for advice.

Do you have a set menu? | **Est-ce que vous avez un menu à prix fixe?**
es kuh vooz avay uñ muhnoo a pree feeks

We will have the menu at ... francs | **Le menu à ... (see NUMBERS) francs**
luh muhnoo a ... froñ

May we see the wine list, please? | **La carte des vins, s'il vous plaît**
la kart day vañ seel voo pleh

What do you recommend? | **Qu'est-ce que vous nous conseillez?**
kes kuh voo noo koñsay-yay

Is there a local speciality? | **Est-ce qu'il y a une spécialité régionale?**
es keel ya oon spay-syalee-tay ray-zhonal

How is this dish served? | **Ce plat est servi comment?**
suh pla eh sehrvee komoñ

How do I eat this? | **Comment ça se mange?**
komoñ sa suh moñzh

What is in this dish? | **Ce plat est préparé avec quoi?**
suh pla eh praypa-ray avek kwah

Are the vegetables included? | **Est-ce que les légumes sont compris?**
es kuh lay laygoom soñ koñpree

Rare/medium rare/well done | **Saignant/Pas trop cuit/Bien cuit**
say-nyoñ/pa troh kwee/byañ kwee

We'd like a dessert/some coffee, please | **Les desserts/Du café, s'il vous plaît**
lay dessehr/doo kafay seel voo pleh

See also **COMPLAINTS, EATING OUT, PAYING, WINES & SPIRITS**

Streetwise

VAT (TVA) is usually included in prices: the rate is 18.6%. A TTC price is a price which includes all taxes. Major international credit cards, Eurocheques (supported by a valid card) and travellers' cheques are widely accepted.

Can I have the bill, please?	**L'addition, s'il vous plaît** *ladee-syoñ seel voo pleh*
Is service/tax included?	**Est-ce que le service est compris?/Est-ce que la taxe est comprise?** *es kuh luh sehrvees eh koñpree/es kuh la tax eh koñpreez*
What does that come to?	**Ça fait combien?** *sa feh koñ-byañ*
Do I pay in advance?	**Est-ce que c'est payable d'avance?** *es kuh say pay-yabl davoñs*
Do I pay a deposit?	**Est-ce qu'il y a des arrhes à verser?** *es keel ya dayz ar a vehrsay*
Can I pay by credit card/cheque?	**Est-ce qu'il est possible de payer avec une carte de crédit/par chèque?** *es keel eh po-seebl duh pay-yay avek oon kart duh kraydee/par shek*
Do you accept traveller's cheques?	**Est-ce que vous acceptez les travellers?** *es kuh vooz aksep-tay lay trav-lurz*
I think you've given me the wrong change	**Je crois que vous ne m'avez pas rendu juste** *zhuh krwah kuh voo nuh mavay pa roñdoo zhoost*
I'd like a receipt, please	**Un reçu, s'il vous plaît** *uñ ruhsoo seel voo pleh*

See also **BUYING, MONEY**

PERSONAL DETAILS

My name is ...	**Je m'appelle ...** *zhuh mapel ...*
My date of birth is 12th February 1949	**Je suis né le 12 février 1949** *zhuh swee nay luh dooz fayvree-ay meel nuf soñ karoñt-nuf*
My address is ...	**J'habite ...** *zhabeet ...*
I come from Britain/America	**Je suis Britannique/Américain** *zhuh swee breetaneek/amayree-kañ*
I live in Manchester/Scotland	**J'habite à Manchester/en Ecosse** *zhabeet a manchester/oñn aykos*
My passport/driving licence number is ...	**Le numéro de mon passeport/permis de conduire est ...** *luh noomay-roh duh moñ paspor/pehrmee duh koñdweer eh ...*
I work in an office/a factory	**Je travaille dans un bureau/une usine** *zhuh travye doñz uñ booroh/oon oozeen*
I am a secretary/manager	**Je suis secrétaire/directeur** *zhuh swee suhkray-tehr/deerek-tur*
I'm here on holiday/business	**Je suis ici en vacances/en voyage d'affaires** *zhuh swee eesee oñ vakoñs/oñ vwah-yazh dafehr*
There are four of us altogether	**Nous sommes quatre** *noo som katr*
My daughter/My son is six	**Ma fille/Mon fils a six ans** *ma feey/moñ fees a seez oñ*

20 litres of
unleaded petrol

20 litres d'essence sans plomb
vañ leetr dessoñs soñ ploñ

100 francs' (worth)
of 4 star, please

100 francs de super, s'il vous plaît
soñ froñ duh soopehr seel voo pleh

Fill it up, please

Le plein, s'il vous plaît
luh plañ seel voo pleh

Check the oil/the
water, please

Vérifiez l'huile/l'eau, s'il vous plaît
vayree-fee-ay lweel/loh seel voo pleh

Top up the windscreen
washers

Remplissez les lave-glaces
roñplee-say lay lavglas

Could you clean the
windscreen?

Faites le pare-brise, s'il vous plaît
fet luh parbreez seel voo pleh

Where's the air line?

**Où se trouve le manomètre pour la
pression des pneus?**
*oo suh troov luh mano-metr poor la preh-syoñ
day pnuh*

Can I have a can of
petrol/oil?

Un bidon d'essence/d'huile, s'il vous plaît
uñ beedoñ dessoñs/dweel seel voo pleh

Is there a telephone/
a lavatory?

Est-ce qu'il y a un téléphone/des toilettes?
es keel ya uñ taylay-fon/day twalet

How do I use the
car wash?

Comment marche le lave-auto?
komoñ marsh luh lav-ohtoh

Can I pay by credit
card?

**Est-ce que je peux payer avec une carte
de crédit?**
*es kuh zhuh puh pay-yay avek oon kart duh
kraydee*

See also **DRIVING, PAYING**

PHOTOGRAPHY

Streetwise

I need a colour/black and white film for this camera	**Je voudrais un film couleur/noir et blanc pour cet appareil** *zhuh voodray uñ feelm koo-lur/nwahr ay bloñ poor set apa-ray*
It is for prints/slides	**C'est pour des photos sur papier/des diapositives** *say poor day foto soor papyay/day dyapo-zee-teev*
Have you got some flash cubes for this camera?	**Avez-vous des flashs pour cet appareil?** *avay-voo day flash poor set apa-ray*
The film/shutter has jammed	**Le film/L'obturateur est bloqué** *luh feelm/loptoo-ratur eh blokay*
Can you develop this film?	**Pouvez-vous développer ce film?** *poovay-voo day-vlopay suh feelm*
When will the photos be ready?	**Les photos seront prêtes quand?** *lay foto suhroñ pret koñ*
Can I take photos in here?	**Est-ce que je peux prendre des photos, ici?** *es kuh zhuh puh proñdr day foto eesee*
Would you take a photo of us, please?	**Est-ce que vous pourriez prendre une photo de nous, s'il vous plaît?** *es kuh voo pooree-ay proñdr oon foto duh noo seel voo pleh*

We should call the police	**Nous devrions appeler la police** *noo duh-vryoñ aplay la polees*
Where is the police station?	**Où est le poste de police?** *oo eh luh post duh polees*
Some things have been stolen from my car	**On a volé des choses dans ma voiture** *oñ a volay day shohz doñ ma vwatoor*
I've been robbed	**On m'a volé quelque chose** *oñ ma volay kelkuh shohz*
I have had an accident	**J'ai eu un accident** *zhay oo uñn aksee-doñ*
How much is the fine?	**L'amende est de combien?** *lamoñd eh duh koñ-byañ*
How do I pay it?	**Comment est-ce que je la paie?** *komoñ es kuh zhuh la peh*
I don't have my driving licence on me	**Je n'ai pas mon permis de conduire sur moi** *zhuh nay pa moñ pehrmee duh koñdweer soor mwah*
I'm very sorry, officer	**Je suis désolé, monsieur** *zhuh swee dayzo-lay muhsyuh*

See also **ACCIDENTS, CUSTOMS & PASSPORTS, EMERGENCIES**

Streetwise

At most post offices you will find public telephones with special services for long-distance calls. Stamps are either tarif normal *(first class) or* tarif réduit *(second class). They can also be bought in tobacconists', hotels and newsagents'.*

How much is a letter to England/America?	**C'est combien pour envoyer une lettre en Angleterre/Amérique?** *say koñ-byañ poor oñvwah-yay oon letr oñn oñgluh-tehr/amay-reek*
Six stamps for postcards to Britain, please	**Six timbres pour cartes postales pour la Grande-Bretagne, s'il vous plaît** *see tañbr poor kart pos-tal poor la groñd-bruhta-nyuh seel voo pleh*
Twelve …-franc stamps, please	**Douze timbres à … francs, s'il vous plaît** *dooz tañbr a … froñ seel voo pleh*
I want to send a telegram to Scotland	**Je voudrais envoyer un télégramme en Écosse** *zhuh voodray oñvwah-yay uñ taylay-gram oñn aykos*
When will it arrive?	**Ça arrivera quand?** *sa aree-vuhra koñ*
How much will it cost?	**Ça coûte combien?** *sa koot koñ-byañ*
I want to send this parcel	**Je voudrais envoyer ce paquet** *zhuh voodray oñvwah-yay suh pakay*
I'd like to make a telephone call	**Je voudrais téléphoner** *zhuh voodray taylay-fonay*

Can you help me, please?
Est-ce que vous pouvez m'aider, s'il vous plaît?
es kuh voo poovay meday seel voo pleh

What is the matter?
Qu'est-ce qu'il y a?
kes keel ya

I am in trouble
J'ai un problème
zhay uñ prob-lem

I don't understand
Je ne comprends pas
zhuh nuh koñproñ pa

Do you speak English?
Est-ce que vous parlez anglais?
es kuh voo parlay oñgleh

Please repeat that
Répétez, s'il vous plaît
raypay-tay seel voo pleh

I have run out of money
Je n'ai plus d'argent
zhuh nay ploo dar-zhoñ

My son is lost
Mon fils a disparu
moñ fees a deespa-roo

I have lost my way
Je me suis perdu
zhuh muh swee pehrdoo

I have forgotten my passport
J'ai oublié mon passeport
zhay ooblee-ay moñ paspor

Please give me my passport back
Mon passeport, s'il vous plaît
moñ paspor seel voo pleh

Where is the British Consulate?
Où est le consulat britannique?
oo eh luh koñsoo-la breetaneek

See also **ACCIDENTS, COMPLAINTS, EMERGENCIES, POLICE**

PRONUNCIATION

In the pronunciation system used in this book, French sounds are represented by spellings of the nearest possible sounds in English. Hence, when you read out the pronunciation, given in italics, sound the letters as if you were reading an English word. The following notes should help you:

REPRESENTATION	REMARKS	EXAMPLE	PRONUNCIATION
e/eh	As in met	**sec**	sek
u/uh	As in thud	**repas**	ruhpa
oh	As in go, low	**bateau**	batoh
o	As in dot	**colle**	kol
oñ	Nasalized: let air	**restaurant**	resto-roñ
añ	out through the	**pain**	pañ
uñ	nose as well as	**lundi**	luñdee
	the mouth		
zh	As in measure	**rouge**	roozh
y	As in yet	**pied**	pyay
ye	As in fry	**travailler**	tra-vye-yay
ny	As in companion	**signal**	see-nyal
s	As in sit	**police**	polees

Pronouncing French words from their spelling can be made easier by following some fairly precise 'rules'. Final consonants are often silent:

SPELLING	REPRESENTATION	SPELLING	REPRESENTATION
à, â	a/ah	**ou, oû, u**	oo
e	e/eh (see above)	**ui, uî**	wee
	uh (see above)	**y**	ee
é	ay	**g (+e/i), j**	zh (see above)
è, ê	e/eh (see above)	**gn**	ny (see above)
i, î	ee	**ch**	sh
ô	o (see above)	**th**	t
û	oo	**tion**	syoñ (see above)
ç	s (see above)	**qu**	k
au(x), eau(x)	oh (see above)	**h**	silent
eu(x), œ(u)	uh (see above)	**ll**	sometimes y
oi, oî, oy	wa/wah		(see above)

Streetwise

If you are travelling in Switzerland, remember that each canton (district) has its own local holidays.

New Year's Day	January 1st
Good Friday	*(Switzerland only)*
Easter Monday	
Labour Day	May 1st *(not Switzerland)*
Ascension Day	
Whit Monday	
Bastille Day	July 14th *(France only)*
National Holiday	July 21st *(Belgium only)*
Assumption	August 15th *(not Switzerland)*
All Saint's Day	November 1st *(not Switzerland)*
Armistice Day	November 11th *(not Switzerland)*
Christmas Day	December 25th
St Stephen's Day	December 26th *(not France)*

Streetwise

Children under ten pay half fare and those under four travel free. At the platform entrance the sign 'N'oubliez pas de composter votre billet' indicates the automatic machine into which tickets should be inserted for date-stamping.

What time are the trains to ...?	**À quelle heure sont les trains pour ...?** *a kel ur soñ lay trañ poor ...*
When is the next train to ...?	**À quelle heure est le prochain train pour ...?** *a kel ur eh luh prochañ trañ poor ...*
What time does it get there?	**Il arrive à quelle heure?** *eel areev a kel ur*
Do I have to change?	**Est-ce que je dois changer?** *es kuh zhuh dwah shoñ-zhay*
A return/single to ..., first/second class	**Un aller-retour/Un aller simple pour ..., en première/seconde classe** *uñn alay-ruhtoor/uñn alay sañpl poor ... oñ pruh-myehr/suhgoñd klas*
I want to book a seat in a non-smoking compartment	**Je voudrais réserver une place dans un compartiment non-fumeur** *zhuh voodray rayzehr-vay oon plas doñz uñ koñpar-teemoñ noñ-foomur*
I want to reserve a couchette/sleeper	**Je voudrais réserver une couchette/une place de voiture-lit** *zhuh voodray rayzehr-vay oon kooshet/oon plas duh vwatoor-lee*
Which platform for the train to...?	**Pour ..., c'est quel quai?** *poor ... say kel kay*

See also **LUGGAGE, TRAIN TRAVEL**

REPAIRS

I have broken the window	**J'ai cassé la fenêtre** *zhay kassay la fuhnetr*
There is a hole in these trousers	**Il y a un trou dans ce pantalon** *eel ya uñ troo doñ suh poñta-loñ*
This is broken/torn	**C'est cassé/déchiré** *say kassay/dayshee-ray*
Can you repair this?	**Pouvez-vous réparer ça?** *poovay-voo raypa-ray sa*
Can you repair it quickly?	**Pouvez-vous le réparer rapidement?** *poovay-voo luh raypa-ray rapeed-moñ*
When can you get it done by?	**Vous pouvez le faire pour quand?** *voo poovay luh fehr poor koñ*
I need some glue/a safety pin	**J'ai besoin de colle/d'une épingle de sûreté** *zhay buhzwañ duh kol/doon ay-pañgl duh soortay*
The stitching has come undone	**Les piqûres se sont défaites** *lay peekoor suh soñ dayfet*
Can you reheel these shoes?	**Pouvez-vous remettre un talon à ces chaussures?** *poovay-voo ruhmetr uñ taloñ a say shohsoor*
The screw has come loose	**La vis s'est défaite** *la vees seh dayfet*
The handle has come off	**La poignée s'est détachée** *la pwah-nyay seh dayta-shay*

See also **ACCIDENTS, BREAKDOWNS, EMERGENCIES**

ROAD CONDITIONS

Streetwise

Minor roads signposted with green arrows offer excellent alternative routes when traffic reaches its peak during the summer. In snowy weather studded snow tyres or chains may be compulsory. Remember that on the motorway you will have to pay a toll.

Is there a route that avoids the traffic?	**Est-ce qu'il y a un itinéraire qui évite les encombrements?** *es keel ya uñn eetee-nayrehr kee ayveet layz oñkoñ-bruhmoñ*
Is the traffic heavy on the motorway?	**Est-ce qu'il y a beaucoup de circulation sur l'autoroute?** *es keel ya bohkoo duh seerkoo-la-syoñ soor lohtoh-root*
What is causing this hold-up?	**Quelle est la cause de ce bouchon?** *kel eh la kohz duh suh booshoñ*
When will the road be clear?	**La route sera dégagée dans combien de temps?** *la root suhra dayga-zhay doñ koñ-byañ duh toñ*
Is there a detour?	**Est-ce qu'il y a une déviation?** *es keel ya oon day-vya-syoñ*
Is the road to ... snowed up?	**Est-ce que la route de ... est enneigée?** *es kuh la root duh ... et oñ-neh-zhay*
Is the pass/tunnel open?	**Est-ce que le col/tunnel est ouvert?** *es kuh luh kol/too-nel et oovehr*
Do I need chains/ studded tyres?	**Est-ce que les chaînes/les pneus cloutés sont nécessaires?** *es kuh lay shen/lay pnuh klootay soñ naysay-sehr*

See also **DRIVING, WEATHER**

ROOM SERVICE

Come in!	**Entrez!** *oñtray*
We'd like breakfast/ a bottle of wine in our room	**Nous voudrions le petit déjeuner/une bouteille de vin dans notre chambre** *noo voodree-oñ luh puhtee day-zhuh-nay/oon bootay duh vañ doñ notr shoñbr*
Put it on my bill	**Mettez-le sur ma note** *metay-luh soor ma not*
I'd like an outside line	**C'est pour une communication extérieure** *say poor oon komoo-neeka-syoñ ekstay-ree-ur*
I have lost my key	**J'ai perdu ma clé** *zhay pehrdoo ma klay*
I have locked myself out of my room	**Je me suis enfermé dehors** *zhuh muh swee oñfehr-may duh-or*
I need a hairdryer/ an iron	**J'ai besoin d'un sèche-cheveux/d'un fer à repasser** *zhay buhzwañ duñ sesh-shuhvuh/duñ fehr a ruh-passay*
May I have an extra blanket/pillow?	**Est-ce que je peux avoir une couverture/ un oreiller supplémentaire?** *es kuh zhuh puh avwahr oon koovehr-toor/uñn oray-yay sooplay-moñtehr*
The TV/radio does not work	**La télé/radio ne marche pas** *la taylay/radyo nuh marsh pa*
Please send someone to collect my luggage	**Vous voulez bien envoyer quelqu'un pour prendre mes bagages** *voo voolay byañ oñvwa-yay kelkuñ poor proñdr may bagazh*

See also **CLEANING, COMPLAINTS, HOTEL DESK, TELEPHONE**

SELF-CATERING

Streetwise

You won't find a kettle in a self-catering apartment, so be prepared to boil water in a saucepan. You will need an adaptor-plug for any electrical goods you take with you, but the voltage is the same as in the UK.

We've booked an apartment in the name of ...	**Nous avons réservé un appartement au nom de ...** *nooz avoñ rayzehr-vay uññ apart-moñ oh noñ duh ...*
Could you please show us round?	**Est-ce que vous pourriez nous faire visiter?** *es kuh voo pooree-ay noo fehr veezee-tay*
Where is the electricity meter?	**Où se trouve le compteur électrique?** *oo suh troov luh koñtur aylek-treek*
How does the heating/ the shower work?	**Le chauffage/La douche marche comment?** *luh shohfazh/la doosh marsh komoñ*
When does the cleaner come?	**La femme de ménage vient quand?** *la fam duh maynazh vyañ koñ*
Is the cost of electricity included in the rental?	**Est-ce que l'électricité est comprise dans la location?** *es kuh laylek-treesee-tay eh koñpreez doñ la loka-syoñ*
Is there any extra bedding?	**Est-ce qu'il y a des couvertures supplémentaires?** *es keel ya day koovehr-toor sooplay-moñtehr*
Where can I contact you?	**Où est-ce que je peux vous contacter?** *oo es kuh zhuh puh voo koñtak-tay*

Streetwise

*Generally shops are open 0900-1200 and 1500-1900 Mon. - Sat.,
though many of the larger stores remain open at lunchtime. Some
shops are closed on Mondays. For bargains in clothing, food and
other goods, try the markets – most towns have at least one regularly.*

Where is the main shopping area?	**Où se trouvent la plupart des magasins?** *oo suh troov la ploopar day maga-zañ*
What time do the shops close?	**Les magasins ferment à quelle heure?** *lay maga-zañ fehrm a kel ur*
How much does that cost?	**Ça coûte combien?** *sa koot koñ-byañ*
How much is it per kilo/per metre?	**Ça fait combien le kilo/le mètre?** *sa feh koñ-byañ luh keeloh/luh metr*
Can I try it on?	**Est-ce que je peux l'essayer?** *es kuh zhuh puh lessay-yay*
Where is the shoe/ food department?	**Où est le rayon des chaussures/ d'alimentation?** *oo eh luh ray-yoñ day shohsoor/ dalee-moñta-syoñ*
I'm looking for a gift for my wife	**Je cherche un cadeau pour ma femme** *zhuh shersh uñ kadoh poor ma fam*
I'm just looking	**Je regarde seulement** *zhuh ruhgard suhlmoñ*
Can I have a carrier bag, please?	**Puis-je avoir un sac en plastique?** *pweezh avwahr uñ sak oñ plasteek*

See also **BUYING, PAYING**

SIGHTSEEING

Streetwise

What is there to see here?
Qu'est-ce qu'il y a à voir dans la région?
kes keel ya a vwahr doñ la ray-zhoñ

Excuse me, how do I get to the cathedral?
Pardon, pour la cathédrale s'il vous plaît?
pardoñ poor la katay-dral seel voo pleh

Where is the museum/the main square?
Le musée/La place centrale, s'il vous plaît?
luh moozay/la plas soñtral seel voo pleh

What time does the guided tour begin?
La visite guidée commence à quelle heure?
la veezeet geeday komoñs a kel ur

What time does the museum open?
Le musée ouvre à quelle heure?
luh moozay oovr a kel ur

Is the castle open to the public?
Est-ce que le château est ouvert au public?
es kuh luh shatoh eh oovehr oh poobleek

How much does it cost to get in?
L'entrée coûte combien?
loñtray koot koñbyañ

Can we take photographs here?
C'est permis de prendre des photos?
say pehrmee duh proñdr day foto

Where can I buy a film/some ice cream?
Où est-ce que je peux acheter un film/des glaces?
oo es kuh zhuh puh ashtay uñ feelm/day glas

See also **MAPS & GUIDES, TRIPS & EXCURSIONS**

Do you mind if I smoke?

Ça vous dérange si je fume?
sa voo dayroñzh see zhuh foom

May I have an ashtray?

Un cendrier, s'il vous plaît
uñ soñdree-ay seel voo pleh

Is this a no-smoking area?

Est-ce que c'est une zone non-fumeur?
es kuh say oon zon noñ-foomur

A packet of ..., please

Un paquet de ..., s'il vous plaît
uñ pakay duh ... seel voo pleh

Have you got any American/English cigarettes?

Est-ce que vous avez des cigarettes américaines/anglaises?
es kuh vooz avay day seega-ret amayree-ken/oñglez

Do you have any matches/pipe cleaners?

Avez-vous des allumettes/des cure-pipes?
avay-voo dayz aloo-met/day koor-peep

Have you a refill for my lighter?

Avez-vous une recharge pour mon briquet?
avay-voo oon ruhsharzh poor moñ breekay

Have you got a light?

Avez-vous du feu?
avay-voo doo fuh

SPORTS

Which sports activities are available here?	**On peut pratiquer quels sports, ici?** *oñ puh pratee-kay kel spor eesee*
Is it possible to go riding?	**Est-ce qu'on peut faire du cheval?** *es koñ puh fehr doo shuhval*
Where can we play tennis/golf?	**Où est-ce qu'on peut jouer au tennis/golf?** *oo es koñ puh zhoo-ay oh tenees/golf*
Is there a swimming pool?	**Est-ce qu'il y a une piscine?** *es keel ya oon peeseen*
Are there any interesting walks nearby?	**Est-ce qu'il y a de belles promenades à faire près d'ici?** *es keel ya duh bel prom-nad a fehr preh deesee*
Can we rent the equipment?	**Est-ce qu'on peut louer l'équipement?** *es koñ puh loo-ay laykeep-moñ*
How much does it cost per hour?	**C'est combien l'heure?** *say koñ-byañ lur*
Do we need to be members?	**Est-ce qu'il faut être membre?** *es keel foh etr moñbr*
Where do we buy our tickets?	**Où est-ce qu'on achète les billets?** *oo es koñ a-shet lay bee-yay*
Can we take lessons?	**Est-ce qu'on peut prendre des leçons?** *es koñ puh proñdr day luhsoñ*

See also **BEACH, ENTERTAINMENT, WATERSPORTS, WINTER SPORTS**

Streetwise

You can phone for a taxi, or hail one provided you are not within 50 metres of a taxi rank. The tip should be 15-20% of the total fare.

Can you order me a taxi, please?	**Pouvez-vous m'appeler un taxi, s'il vous plaît?** *poovay-voo maplay uñ taksee seel voo pleh*
To the main station/the airport, please	**À la gare/l'aéroport, s'il vous plaît** *a la gar/la-ehro-por seel voo pleh*
Take me to this address/this hotel	**À cette adresse/cet hôtel, s'il vous plaît** *a set a-dress/set ohtel seel voo pleh*
Is it far?	**Est-ce que c'est loin?** *es kuh say lwañ*
How much will it cost?	**Ça va faire combien?** *sa va fehr koñ-byañ*
I'm in a hurry	**Je suis pressé** *zhuh swee pressay*
Can you wait here for a few minutes?	**Est-ce que vous pouvez m'attendre ici quelques instants?** *es kuh voo poovay ma-toñdr eesee kelkuhz añstoñ*
Please stop here/at the corner	**Arrêtez-vous ici/au coin** *areh-tay-voo eesee/oh kwañ*
How much is it?	**Ça fait combien?** *sa feh koñ-byañ*
Keep the change	**Gardez la monnaie** *garday la monay*

See also **TIPPING**

Streetwise

As soon as you can, buy a phonecard (une télécarte) at a post office. These are available in different numbers of units. They are very convenient, as more and more public phones take only phonecards. However, you should still be able to find phones which accept coins, although some older phones in cafés require tokens (jetons - zhuton) which can be bought at a bar. In phone booths the money is inserted before dialling, coins being refunded if you hang up without getting through. For international calls dial 19 followed by your country code (44 for Britain).

Can I have a line to ...?	**Je voudrais appeler ...** *zhuh voodray aplay ...*
I want to make a phone call	**Je voudrais téléphoner** *zhuh voodray taylay-fonay*
The number is ...	**C'est le numéro ...** (see NUMBERS) *say luh noomay-roh ...*
I want to reverse the charges	**Je voudrais téléphoner en P.C.V.** *zhuh voodray taylay-fonay oñ pay-say-vay*
Have you got change for the phone?	**Avez-vous de la monnaie pour le téléphone?** *avay-voo duh la monay poor luh taylay-fon*
What coins do I need?	**J'ai besoin de quelles pièces?** *zhay buhzwañ duh kel pyess*
How much is it to phone Britain?	**Ça coûte combien pour téléphoner en Grande-Bretagne?** *sa koot koñ-byañ poor taylay-fonay oñ groñd-bruhta-nyuh*
I can't get through	**Je n'arrive pas à obtenir la communication** *zhuh nareev pa a optuh-neer la komoo-neeka-syoñ*

The line's engaged	**C'est occupé** *say okoo-pay*
Hello, this is ...	**Allô, ... à l'appareil** *alo ... a lapa-ray*
Can I speak to ...?	**Est-ce que je peux parler à ...?** *es kuh zhuh puh parlay a ...*
I've been cut off	**Nous avons été coupés** *nooz avoñ aytay koopay*
It's a bad line	**La ligne est mauvaise** *la lee-nyeh movez*

YOU MAY HEAR:

Ne quittez pas! *nuh keetay pa*	I'm trying to connect you/Hold the line
Je vous le passe *zhuh voo luh pas*	I'm putting you through
Je suis désolée, mais la ligne est occupée *zhuh swee dayzoh-lay meh la lee-nyuh eh okoo-pay*	I'm sorry, it's engaged
Est-ce que vous pouvez rappeler plus tard? *es kuh voo poovay raplay ploo tar*	Can you try again later?
C'est de la part de qui? *seh duh la par duh kee*	Who's calling?
Ce n'est pas le bon numéro *suh neh pa luh boñ noomay-roh*	Sorry, wrong number

The 24-hour clock is widely used:

9.00 pm	2100	vingt et une heures
		vañt ay oon ur
4.45 pm	1645	seize heures quarante-cinq
		sez ur karoñt-sañk

What's the time?
Quelle heure est-il?
Kel ur eteel

It's:
Il est:
eel eh

8.00	**huit heures**
	weet ur
8.05	**huit heures cinq**
	weet ur sañk
8.10	**huit heures dix**
	weet ur dees
8.15	**huit heures et quart**
	weet ur ay kar
8.20	**huit heures vingt**
	weet ur vañ
8.25	**huit heures vingt-cinq**
	weet ur vañ-sañk
8.30	**huit heures et demie**
	weet ur ay duhmee
8.35	**neuf heures moins vingt-cinq**
	nuhv ur mwañ vañ-sañk
8.40	**neuf heures moins vingt**
	nuhv ur mwañ vañ
8.45	**neuf heures moins le quart**
	muhv ur mwañ luh kar
8.50	**neuf heures moins dix**
	nuhv ur mwañ dees
8.55	**neuf heures moins cinq**
	nuhv ur mwañ sañk
12.00	**midi** (midday) **minuit** (midnight)
	meedee meenwee

See also **NUMBERS**

What time do you open/close?

Vous ouvrez/Vous fermez à quelle heure?
vooz oovray/voo fehrmay a kel ur

Do we have time to visit the town?

Est-ce que nous avons le temps de visiter la ville?
es kuh nooz avoñ luh toñ duh veezee-tay la veel

How long will it take to get there?

Combien de temps faut-il pour y aller?
koñ-byañ duh toñ foht-eel poor ee alay

We arrived early/late

Nous sommes arrivés en avance/en retard
noo som aree-vay oñn avoñs/oñ ruhtar

We should have been there two hours ago

On aurait dû y être il y a deux heures
oñ oray doo ee etr eel ya duhz ur

We must be back at the hotel before ... o'clock

Il faut être de retour à l'hôtel avant ... heures (*see* TIME)
eel foh etr duh ruhtoor a lohtel avoñ ... ur

When does the coach leave in the morning?

Le car part à quelle heure le matin?
luh kar par a kel ur luh matañ

The tour starts at about ...

La visite guidée commence vers ... (*see* TIME)
la veezeet geeday komoñs vehr ...

The museum is open in the morning/afternoon

Le musée est ouvert le matin/l'après-midi
luh moozay eh oovehr luh matañ/lapray-meedee

The table is booked for ... o'clock this evening

On a réservé une table pour ... heures ce soir (*see* TIME)
oñ a rayzehr-vay oon tabl poor ... ur suh swahr

TIPPING

Streetwise

Most cafés and restaurants include the service charge in the bill, itemised as Service Compris with the relevant percentage shown. If the service charge is not included, (Service Non Compris) you should add between 10 and 15%. Small coins given in the change are usually left for the waiter in any event. Hotel staff (such as the chambermaid and the porter) should also receive a small gratuity.

Sorry, I don't have any change

Je regrette, mais je n'ai pas de monnaie
zhuh ruhgret meh zhuh nay pa duh monay

Could you give me change of ...?

Pourriez-vous me faire la monnaie de ...?
pooree-ay-voo muh fehr la monay duh ...

Is it usual to tip ...?

Est-ce qu'on donne habituellement un pourboire à ...?
es koñ don abee-too-elmoñ uñ poorbwahr a ...

How much should I tip?

Je devrais donner un pourboire de combien?
zhuh duhvray donay uñ poorbwahr duh koñ-byañ

Is the tip included?

Est-ce que le service est compris?
es kuh luh sehrvees eh koñpree

Keep the change

Gardez la monnaie
garday la monay

Make it ...

Rendez-moi sur ... (*see* NUMBERS)
roñday-mwah soor ...

See also **TAXIS, TOILETS**

Toilets are usually of a high standard when maintained by an attendant (who should be tipped at least one franc). In the cities you can now find coin-operated 'superloos': these are particularly hygienic as the whole booth is automatically sterilised each time it is used.

Where are the toilets, please?
Les toilettes, s'il vous plaît?
lay twalet seel voo pleh

Do you have to pay?
Est-ce qu'il faut payer?
es keel foh pay-yay

This toilet does not flush
La chasse d'eau ne marche pas
la shas doh nuh marsh pa

There is no toilet paper/soap
Il n'y a pas de papier hygiénique/de savon
eel nya pa duh papyay ee-zhyay-neek/duh savoñ

Is there a toilet for the disabled?
Est-ce qu'il y a des toilettes pour handicapés?
es keel ya day twalet poor oñdee-kapay

Is there somewhere I can change the baby?
Est-ce qu'il y a un endroit pour changer le bébé?
es keel ya uñn oñdrwah poor shoñ-zhay luh baybay

The towels have run out
Les essuie-mains sont finis
layz eswee-mañ soñ feenee

The door will not close
La porte ne ferme pas
la port nuh fehrm pa

TRAIN TRAVEL

Streetwise

There are three categories of regular trains: Omnibus, Rapide and Express, from the slowest to the quickest. All are usually clean and punctual. The fastest train in France is the TGV which links Paris and Marseilles. Seats on the TGV have to be booked in advance and a supplement has to be paid. For all trains, booking is always advisable, especially on night trains with sleepers.

Is this the train for ...?	**Est-ce que c'est le train pour ...?** *es kuh say luh trañ poor ...*
Is this seat free?	**Est-ce que cette place est libre?** *es kuh set plas eh leebr*
May I open the window?	**Est-ce que je peux ouvrir la fenêtre?** *es kuh zhuh puh oovreer la fuhnetr*
What time do we get to ...?	**Nous arrivons à quelle heure à ...?** *nooz aree-voñ a kel ur a ...*
Do we stop at ...?	**Est-ce que le train s'arrête à ...?** *es kuh luh trañ saret a ...*
Where do I change for ...?	**Où est-ce que je change pour aller à ...?** *oo es kuh zhuh shoñzh poor alay a ...*
Is there a buffet car/ restaurant car?	**Est-ce qu'il y a un buffet/wagon-restaurant?** *es keel ya uñ boofay/vagoñ-resto-roñ*
This is a no-smoking compartment	**Ici, c'est un compartiment non-fumeur** *eesee say uñ koñpar-teemoñ noñ-foomur*
Please tell me when we get to ...	**Dites-moi, s'il vous plaît, lorsque nous serons à ...** *deet-mwah seel voo pleh lorskuh noo suhroñ a ...*

See also **LUGGAGE, RAILWAY STATION, TRAVEL AGENT**

What's the best way to get to ...?	**Quelle est la meilleure façon pour aller à ...?** *kel eh la may-yur fasoñ poor alay a ...*
How much is it to fly to ...?	**Ça coûte combien pour aller en avion à ...?** *sa koot koñ-byañ poor alay oñn-a-vyoñ a ...*
Are there any special cheap fares?	**Est-ce qu'il existe des tarifs réduits spéciaux?** *es keel egzeest day tareef raydwee spay-syoh*
What times are the trains/flights?	**Quel est l'horaire des trains/vols?** *kel eh lorehr day trañ/vol*
Can I buy the tickets here?	**Est-ce que je peux acheter les billets ici?** *es kuh zhuh puh ashtay lay bee-yay eesee*
Can I change my booking?	**Est-ce que je peux changer ma réservation?** *es kuh zhuh puh shoñ-zhay ma rayzehr-va-syoñ*
Can you book me on the London flight?	**Pouvez-vous me réserver une place sur le vol de Londres?** *poovay-voo muh rayzehr-vay oon plas soor luh vol duh loñdr*
Can I get back to Manchester tonight?	**Est-ce que je peux rentrer à Manchester ce soir?** *es kuh zhuh puh roñtray a manchester suh swahr*
Two second class returns to ..	**Deux aller-retour en deuxième classe pour ...** *duhz alay-ruhtoor oñ duh-zyem klas poor ...*
Can you book me into a hotel?	**Pouvez-vous me réserver une chambre dans un hôtel?** *poovay-voo muh rayzehr-vay oon shoñbr doñz uññ ohtel*

Streetwise

For information, go to the local tourist office (syndicat d'initiative).

Are there any sightseeing tours?	**Y a-t-il des excursions organisées?** *ee ateel dayz ekskoor-syoñ orga-neezay*
When is the bus tour of the town?	**La visite guidée de la ville en bus est à quelle heure?** *la veezeet geeday duh la veel oñ boos eh a kel ur*
How long does the tour take?	**La visite dure combien de temps?** *la veezeet door koñ-byañ duh toñ*
Are there any boat trips on the river/lake?	**Y a-t-il des excursions en bateau sur la rivière/le lac?** *ee ateel dayz ekskoor-syoñ oñ batoh soor la ree-vyehr/luh lak*
Is there a guided tour of the cathedral?	**Est-ce qu'il y a une visite guidée de la cathédrale?** *es keel ya oon veezeet geeday duh la katay-dral*
Is there a reduction for children/senior citizens/a group?	**Y a-t-il une réduction pour les enfants/les retraités/un groupe?** *ee ateel oon raydook-syoñ poor layz oñfoñ/lay ruhtreh-tay/uñ groop*
Is there a commentary in English?	**Est-ce qu'il y a un commentaire en anglais?** *es keel ya uñ komoñ-tehr oñn oñgleh*
Please stop the bus, my child is feeling sick!	**Arrêtez le bus, s'il vous plaît, mon enfant a mal au cœur!** *areh-tay luh boos seel voo pleh mon oñfoñ a mal oh kur*

See also **SIGHTSEEING**

Streetwise

The police will give you information on permits for sailing and fishing.

Is it possible to go water-skiing/ windsurfing	**Est-il possible de faire du ski nautique/de la planche à voile?** *ehteel po-seebl duh fehr doo skee nohteek/duh la ploñsh a vwahl*
Can we rent a motor boat/rowing boat?	**Est-ce qu'on peut louer un bateau à moteur/bateau à rames?** *es koñ puh loo-ay uñ batoh a mo-tur/batoh a ram*
Can I rent a sailboard?	**Est-ce qu'on peut louer une planche à voile?** *es koñ puh loo-ay oon ploñsh a vwahl*
Can one swim in the river?	**Peut-on se baigner dans la rivière?** *puht-oñ suh bay-nyay doñ la ree-vyehr*
Can we fish here?	**Est-ce qu'on peut pêcher ici?** *es koñ puh payshay eesee*
Is there a paddling pool for the children?	**Est-ce qu'il y a un petit bain pour les enfants?** *es keel ya uñ puhtee bañ poor layz oñfoñ*
Where is the municipal swimming pool?	**Où est la piscine municipale?** *oo eh la peeseen moonee-seepal*
Is the pool heated?	**Est-ce que la piscine est chauffée?** *es kuh la peeseen eh shohfay*
Is it an outdoor pool?	**Est-ce que c'est une piscine en pleine air?** *es kuh say oon peeseen oñ plen ehr*

See also **BEACH, SAILING**

Streetwise

Ask at the local tourist office for details of special weather bulletins for hikers and sailors.

It's a lovely day!	**Qu'il fait beau!** *keel feh boh*
What dreadful weather!	**Quel temps affreux!** *kel toñ afruh*
It is raining/snowing	**Il pleut/neige** *eel pluh/nezh*
It's windy/sunny/foggy	**Il fait du vent/du soleil/du brouillard** *eel feh doo voñ/doo solay/doo broo-yar*
There's a nice breeze blowing	**Il y a une petite brise agréable** *eel ya oon puhteet breez agray-abl*
Will it be cold tonight?	**Est-ce qu'il va faire froid cette nuit?** *es keel va fehr frwa set nwee*
Is it going to rain/to snow?	**Est-ce qu'il va pleuvoir/neiger?** *es keel va pluhvwahr/neh-zhay*
Will there be a thunderstorm?	**Est-ce qu'il va y avoir un orage?** *es keel va ee avwahr uñn orazh*
Is it going to be fine?	**Est-ce qu'il va faire beau?** *es keel va fehr boh*
Is the weather going to change?	**Est-ce que le temps va changer?** *es kuh luh toñ va shoñ-zhay*
What is the temperature?	**Quelle est la température?** *kel eh la toñpay-ratoor*

From the point of view of quality, France remains the most important wine-producing country in the world. Its major wine-producing regions are:

la Champagne (an area which produces only champagne);
l'Alsace (white, mainly dry, wines);
la Bourgogne (mainly high-quality red wines);
le Beaujolais (red wines);
les Côtes du Rhône (good value red, white and rosé);
le Languedoc-Roussillon (good value red and rosé);
les Côtes de Provence (mainly red but also rosé);
the Bordeaux region (mainly red plus some sweet whites);
the Loire valley (red and dry white wines).

In restaurants, house wines served in carafes are often excellent and you can ask for quite small amounts – quarter- or half-litre carafes. Otherwise, a guide to the quality of French wines is provided by the wine control system adopted nationally. This indicates the level of control imposed on the production of the wine and on the quality of the grapes used. There are three categories:

Appellation d'origine contrôlée (AC) – the highest classification. This indicates that very strict controls have been imposed on the production of the wine and that only the best grapes have been used.

Vin délimité de qualité supériéure (VDQS) – the intermediate category.

Vin de pays (VDP) – the lowest category of classified wines, obviously inferior to the above but generally of a higher quality than unclassified ordinary wines (normally labelled *vin de table*).

Most well-known brands of spirits are available in France. Among the most popular French drinks is *pastis*, an aniseed-flavoured aperitif normally taken with water – the best-known brands are Pernod and Ricard. If you want to try something a little stronger, ask for a glass of *eau de vie (oh duh vee),* a powerful spirit usually made with fruit.

We'd like an aperitif	**Un apéritif, s'il vous plaît** *uñn apay-reeteef seel voo pleh*
May I have the wine list, please?	**La carte des vins, s'il vous plaît** *la kart day vañ seel voo pleh*
Can you recommend a good red/white/rosé wine?	**Pouvez-vous nous conseiller un bon vin rouge/blanc/rosé?** *poovay-voo noo koñsay-yay uñ boñ vañ roozh/bloñ/rohzay*
A bottle/carafe of house wine	**Une bouteille/carafe de la réserve du patron** *oon bootay/karaf duh la ray-zehrv doo patroñ*
A half bottle	**Une demi-bouteille** *oon duhmee-bootay*
Would you bring another glass, please?	**Un autre verre, s'il vous plaît** *uñn ohtr vehr seel voo pleh*
This wine is not chilled	**Ce vin n'est pas assez frais** *suh vañ neh pa assay freh*
What liqueurs do you have?	**Qu'est-ce que vous avez comme liqueurs?** *kes kuh vooz avay kom lee-kur*
I'll have a brandy/a Scotch	**Un cognac/Un whisky, s'il vous plaît** *uñ koñ-yak/uñ weeskee seel voo pleh*
A gin and tonic	**Un gin-tonic** *uñ djeen-toneek*
A Martini and lemonade	**Un martini avec de la limonade** *uñ martee-nee avek duh la leemo-nad*

See also **DRINKS, EATING OUT, MENUS, ORDERING**

Streetwise

Can we hire skis here?	**Est-ce qu'on peut louer des skis ici?** *es koñ puh loo-ay day skee eesee*
Could you adjust my bindings?	**Pouvez-vous ajuster mes fixations?** *poovay-voo a-zhoostay may feeksa-syoñ*
A one-week pass, please	**Un abonnement d'une semaine, s'il vous plaît** *uñn abon-moñ doon smen seel voo pleh*
What are the snow conditions?	**Quelles sont les conditions d'enneigement?** *kel soñ lay koñdee-syoñ doññezh-moñ*
Is there a restaurant at the top station?	**Y a-t-il un restaurant à la gare supérieure?** *ee ateel uñ resto-roñ a la gar soopay-ryur*
Which are the easiest runs?	**Quelles sont les pistes les plus faciles?** *kel soñ lay peest lay ploo faseel*
When is the last ascent?	**À quelle heure part la dernière benne?** *a kel ur par la dehr-nyehr ben*
Is there danger of avalanches?	**Y a-t-il risque d'avalanche?** *ee ateel reesk dava-loñsh*
Where can we go skating?	**Où est-ce qu'on peut faire du patin?** *oo es koñ puh fehr doo patañ*
Is there a toboggan run?	**Y a-t-il une piste de luge?** *ee ateel oon peest duh loozh*

a un/une *uñ/oon*

abbey l'abbaye *(f) abay-ee*

about: a book about Paris un livre sur Paris *uñ leevr soor pahree*; **about ten o'clock** vers dix heures *vehr dees ur*

above au-dessus *oh-duhsoo*

accident l'accident *(m) aksee-doñ*

accommodation le logement *lozh-moñ*

ache la douleur *doolur*; **my head aches** j'ai mal à la tête *zhay mal a la tet*

adaptor *(electrical)* la prise multiple *preez mool-teepl*

address l'adresse *(f) adress*

adhesive tape le ruban adhésif *rooboñ aday-zeef*

admission charge l'entrée *oñtray*

adult l'adulte *(m/f) adoolt*

advance: in advance à l'avance *a lavoñs*

after après *apray*

afternoon l'après-midi *(m) apray-meedee*

aftershave la lotion après-rasage *loh-syoñ apray-razazh*

again de nouveau *duh noovo*

agent l'agent *(m) a-zhoñ*

ago: a week ago il y a une semaine *eel ya oon smen*

air-conditioning la climatisation *kleema-teeza-syoñ*

air mail par avion *par a-vyoñ*

air-mattress le matelas pneumatique *matla p-nuhma-teek*

airport l'aéroport *(m) a-ehro-por*

aisle le couloir *kool-wahr*

alcohol l'alcool *(m) alkol*

alcoholic alcoolique *alkoleek*

all tout(e)/tous/toutes *too(t)/too/toot*

allergic allergique à *alehr-zheek a*

allowance *(customs)* la quantité tolérée *koñtee-tay tolay-ray*

all right *(agreed)* d'accord *dakor*; **are you all right?** ça va? *sa va*

almost presque *presk*

the Alps les Alpes *alp*

also aussi *ohsee*

always toujours *too-zhoor*

am *see* GRAMMAR

ambulance l'ambulance *(f) oñboo-loñs*

America l'Amérique *(f) amay-reek*

American américain *amayree-kañ*

anaesthetic l'anesthésique *(m) anay-stayseek*

and et *ay*

anorak l'anorak *(m)*

another un(e) autre *uñ/oon ohtr*; **another beer?** encore une bière? *oñkor oon bee-ayr*

antibiotic l'antibiotique *(m) oñtee-byoteek*

antifreeze l'antigel *(m) oñtee-zhel*

antiseptic l'antiseptique *(m) oñtee-septeek*

any: I haven't any je n'en ai pas *zhuh non ay pa*; **have you any apples?** avez-vous des pommes? *avay-voo day pom*

apartment l'appartement *(m) apartmoñ*

aperitif l'apéritif *(m) apay-reeteef*

apple la pomme *pom*

appointment le rendez-vous

roñday-voo

apricot l'abricot *(m) abreeko*

are *see* GRAMMAR

arm le bras *bra*

armbands *(for swimming)* les flotteurs *(mpl)* de natation *flotur duh nata-syoñ*

arrival l'arrivée *(f) aree-vay*

arrive arriver *aree-vay*

art gallery le musée d'art *moozay dar*

artichoke l'artichaut *(m) arteesho*

ashtray le cendrier *soñdree-yay*

asparagus les asperges *(fpl) asperzh*

aspirin l'aspirine *(f) aspee-reen*

asthma l'asthme *(m) asmuh*

at à *a;* **at home** à la maison *a la mayzoñ*

aubergine l'aubergine *(f) ohbehr-zheen*

Australia l'Australie *(f) ostralee*

Australian australien *ostra-lyañ*

automatic automatique *ohto-ma-teek*

autumn l'automne *(m) o-ton*

avalanche l'avalanche *(f) ava-loñsh*

avocado l'avocat *(m) avo-ka*

baby le bébé *baybay*

baby food les petits pots *(mpl) puhtee poh*

babysitter le/la babysitter *baybee-seetehr*

back *(of body)* le dos *doh*

backpack le sac au dos *sak oh doh*

bacon le bacon *baykon*

bad *(food)* gâté *gahtay;* *(weather,*

news) mauvais *moveh*

bag le sac *sak*

baggage les bagages *(mpl) bagazh*

baggage reclaim la réception des bagages *raysep-syoñ day bagazh*

baker's la boulangerie *booloñ-zhuree*

balcony le balcon *balkoñ*

ball la balle *bal*

banana la banane *banan*

band *(musical)* la fanfare *foñ-far*

bandage le pansement *poñsmoñ*

bank la banque *boñk*

bar le bar *bar*

barber le coiffeur *kwa-fur*

basket la corbeille *korbay*

bath la baignoire *bay-nwahr;* **to take a bath** prendre un bain *proñdr uñ bañ*

bathing cap le bonnet de bain *boneh duh bañ*

bathroom la salle de bains *sal duh bañ*

battery *(for car)* la batterie *batree*

be être *etr; see* GRAMMAR

beach la plage *plazh*

bean le haricot *areekoh*

beautiful beau/belle *boh/bel*

bed le lit *lee*

bedding la literie *leetree*

bedroom la chambre à coucher *shoñbr-a kooshay*

beef le boeuf *buhf*

beer la bière *bee-ayr*

beetroot la betterave *betrav*

before avant *avoñ*

begin commencer *komoñ-say*

behind derrière *dehr-yehr*
Belgian belge *belzh*
Belgium la Belgique *bel-zheek*
below sous *soo*
belt la ceinture *sañtoor*
beside à côté de *a kohtay duh*
best meilleur *may-yur*
better mieux *myuh*
between entre *oñtr*
bicycle la bicyclette *beesee-klet*
big grand *groñ*
bigger (than) plus grand (que) *ploo groñ (kuh)*
bikini le bikini *beekee-nee*
bill l'addition (f) *adee-syoñ*
bin la poubelle *poo-bel*
binoculars les jumelles (fpl) *zhoo-mel*
bird l'oiseau (m) *wazoh*
birthday l'anniversaire (m) *anee-vehrsehr*; **happy birthday!** bon anniversaire! *bon anee-vehrsehr*
birthday card la carte d'anniversaire *kart danee-vehrsehr*
bit: a bit (of) un peu (de) *uñ puh (duh)*
bitten mordu *mor-doo*; **(by insect)** piqué *pee-kay*
bitter amer *amehr*
black noir *nwahr*
blackcurrant le cassis *ka-see*
blanket la couverture *koovehr-toor*
bleach l'eau (f) de Javel *oh duh zha-vel*
blocked bouché *booshay*
blood group le groupe sanguin *groop soñgañ*

blouse le chemisier *shuhmee-zyay*
blow-dry le brushing *bruh-sheeng*
blue bleu *bluh*
boarding card la carte d'embarquement *kart doñbark-moñ*
boarding house la pension (de famille) *poñ-syoñ (duh fameey)*
boat le bateau *batoh*
boat trip l'excursion (f) en bateau *ekskoor-syoñ oñ batoh*
boiled bouilli *boo-yee*
book¹ n le livre *leevr*
book² vb réserver *rayzehr-vay*
booking la réservation *rayzehr-va-syoñ*
booking office le bureau de location *booroh duh loka-syoñ*
book of tickets le carnet de tickets *karneh duh teekeh*
bookshop la librairie *leebreh-ree*
boots (to wear) les bottes (fpl) *bot*
border la frontière *froñ-tyehr*
both les deux *lay duh*
bottle la bouteille *bootay*
bottle opener l'ouvre-bouteilles (m) *oovr-bootay*
box la boîte *bwat*
box office le bureau de location *booroh duh loka-syoñ*
boy le garçon *garsoñ*
boyfriend le petit ami *puhteet amee*
bra le soutien-gorge *soo-tyañ gorzh*
bracelet le bracelet *braslay*
brake fluid le liquide pour freins *leekeed poor frañ*
brakes les freins (mpl) *frañ*
brandy le cognac *konyak*

bread le pain *pañ*

breakable fragile *fra-zheel*

breakdown la panne *pan*

breakdown van la dépanneuse *daypa-nuz*

breakfast le petit déjeuner *puhtee day-zhuh-nay*

breast *(chicken)* le blanc *bloñ*

briefcase la serviette *sehr-vyet*

bring apporter *aportay*

Britain la Grande Bretagne *groñd bruhta-nyuh*

British britannique *breetaneek*

brochure la brochure *broshoor*

broken cassé *kassay*

broken down *(machine, car)* en panne *oñ pan*

brooch la broche *brosh*

broom le balai *balay*

brother le frère *frehr*

brown marron *maroñ*

brush la brosse *bros*

Brussels sprouts les choux *(mpl)* de Bruxelles *shoo duh broo-sel*

bucket le seau *soh*

buffet le buffet *boofay*

buffet car le voiture-buffet *vwatoor-boofay*

bulb l'ampoule *(f)* *oñpool*

bus l'autobus *(m)* *ohto-boos*

business les affaires *(fpl)* *afehr*

bus station la gare routière *gar roo-tyehr*

bus stop l'arrêt *(m)* d'autobus *areh dohto-boos*

bus tour l'excursion *(f)* en autobus *ekskoor-syoñ oñ ohto-boos*

busy occupé *okoopay*

but mais *may*

butcher's la boucherie *boosh-ree*

butter le beurre *buhr*

button le bouton *bootoñ*

buy acheter *ashtay*

by *(via)* via *vya*; *(beside)* à côté de *a kotay duh*

bypass la route de contournement *root duh koñtoorn-moñ*

cabaret le cabaret *kabaray*

cabbage le chou *shoo*

cablecar le téléphérique *taylay-fayreek*

café le café *kafay*

cake le gâteau *gato*

call[1] *vb* appeler *apuh-lay*

call[2] *n (on telephone)* l'appel *(m)* a-*pel*; **a long-distance call** le communication interurbaine *komoo-neeka-syoñ añtehr-oor-ben*

calm calme *kalm*

camera l'appareil-photo *(m)* *aparay-fohto*

camp camper *koñpay*

camp site le camping *koñping*

can[1] *n* la boîte *bwat*

can[2] *vb* **: can I ...?** puis-je ...? *pwee-zhuh*

Canada le Canada *kanada*

Canadian canadien *kanadyañ*

cancel annuler *anoolay*

canoe le canoë *kano-eh*

canoeing le *(sport du)* canoë *(spor doo)* *kano-eh*

can opener l'ouvre-boîtes *(m)* *oovr-bwat*

car la voiture *vwatoor*
carafe la carafe *karaf*
caravan la caravane *kara-van*
carburettor le carburateur *karboora-tur*
card la carte *kart*
cardigan le gilet (de laine) *zheelay (duh len)*
careful soigneux *swa-nyuh*
car park le parking *parkeeng*
carpet le tapis *tapee*
carriage (railway) la voiture *vwatoor*
carrot la carotte *karot*
carry porter *portay*
car wash le lave-auto *lav-ohto*
case (suitcase) la valise *valeez*
cash¹ vb (cheque) encaisser *oñkeh-say*
cash² n l'argent (m) liquide *ar-zhoñ leekeed*
cash desk la caisse *kes*
cashier le caissier/la caissière *keh-syay/keh-syehr*
casino le casino *kazee-noh*
cassette la cassette *ka-set*
castle le château *shatoh*
catch attraper *atrapay*
cathedral la cathédrale *katay-dral*
Catholic catholique *kato-leek*
cauliflower le chou-fleur *shoo-flur*
cave la caverne *kavehrn*
celery le céleri *sayl-ree*
cemetery le cimetière *seem-tyehr*
centimetre le centimètre *soñtee-metr*
central central *soñtral*
centre le centre *soñtr*

cereal (for breakfast) les céréales (fpl) *sayray-al*
certain (sure) certain *sehrtañ*
certificate le certificat *sehrteefεe-ka*
chain la chaîne *shen*
chair la chaise *shez*
chairlift le télésiège *taylay-syezh*
chalet le chalet *shalay*
champagne le champagne *shoñpa-nyuh*
change¹ n (money) la monnaie *monay*
change² vb changer *shoñ-zhay*
changing room le salon d'essayage *saloñ dessay-yazh*
chapel la chapelle *sha-pel*
charge le prix *pree*
cheap bon marché *boñ marshay*
cheaper moins cher *mwañ shehr*
check vérifier *vayree-fyay*
check in enregistrer *oñruh-zheestray*
check-in desk l'enregistrement (m) des bagages *oñruh-zheestruh-moñ day bagazh*
cheerio au revoir *oh ruh-vwar*
cheers! à la vôtre *a la vohtr*
cheese le fromage *fromazh*
chemist's la pharmacie *farma-see*
cheque le chèque *shek*
cheque book le carnet de chèques *karneh duh shek*
cheque card la carte d'identité bancaire *kart deedoñ-teetay boñkehr*
cherry la cerise *suhreez*
chestnut la châtaigne *shateh-nyuh*
chewing gum le chewing-gum *shoo-eeng gum*

chicken le poulet *pooleh*

chickenpox la varicelle *varee-sel*

child l'enfant *(m)* *oñfoñ*

children les enfants *oñfoñ*

chilli le piment rouge *peemoñ roozh*

chips les frites *(fpl)* *freet*

chocolate le chocolat *shoko-la*

chocolates les chocolats *shoko-la*

Christmas Noël *(m/f)* *no-el*; **merry Christmas!** joyeux Noël! *zwah-yuh no-el*

church l'église *(f)* *aygleez*

cider le cidre *seedr*

cigar le cigare *seegar*

cigarette papers les papiers *(mpl)* à cigarettes *papyay a seega-ret*

cigarette la cigarette *seega-ret*

cinema le cinéma *seenay-ma*

circus le cirque *seerk*

city la ville *veel*

clean[1] *adj* propre *propr*

clean[2] *vb* nettoyer *netwa-yay*

cleansing cream la crème démaquillante *krem dayma-kee-yoñt*

client le client/la cliente *klee-oñ/klee-oñt*

climbing l'escalade *(f)* *eska-lad*

climbing boots les chaussures *(fpl)* d'escalade *shoh-soor deska-lad*

cloakroom le vestiaire *vest-yehr*

clock l'horloge *(f)* *orlozh*

close[1] *adj* *(near)* proche *prosh*

close[2] *vb* fermer *fehrmay*

closed fermé *fehrmay*

cloth le chiffon *shee-foñ*

clothes les vêtements *(mpl)* *vetmoñ*

clothes peg la pince à linge *pañs a lañzh*

cloudy nuageux *nwa-zhuh*

cloves les clous *(mpl)* de girofle *kloo duh zhee-rofluh*

club le club *klub*

coach *(bus)* l'autobus *(m)* *ohto-boos*; *(train)* la voiture *vwatoor*

coach trip l'excursion *(f)* en car *ekskoor-syoñ oñ kar*

coast la côte *koht*

coastguard le garde-côte *gard-koht*

coat le manteau *moñto*

coat hanger le cintre *sañtr*

cocktail le cocktail *koktel*

cocoa le cacao *kaka-oh*

coconut la noix de coco *nwa duh kohkoh*

coffee le café *kafay*; **white coffee** le café au lait *kafay oh leh*; **black coffee** le café noir *kafay nwahr*

coin la pièce de monnaie *pyes duh monay*

colander la passoire *paswar*

cold froid *frwa*; **I'm cold** j'ai froid *zhay frwa*; **I have a cold** je suis enrhumé *zhuh sweez oñroo-may*

colour la couleur *koo-lur*

comb le peigne *peh-nyuh*

come venir *vuhneer*; **to come back** revenir *ruvneer*; **to come in** entrer *oñtray*; **come in!** entrez! *oñtray*

comfortable confortable *koñfor-tabl*

communion la communion *komoo-nyoñ*

company la compagnie *koñpa-nyee*

compartment le compartiment

koñpar-teemoñ

complain se plaindre *suh plañdr*

compulsory obligatoire *oblee-gatwahr*

computer l'ordinateur *ordeena-tur*

concert le concert *koñsehr*

condensed milk le lait concentré *leh koñsoñ-tray*

conditioner l'après-shampooing *(m) apray-shoñpwañ*

conductor *(on bus)* le receveur *rus-vur*

conference la conférence *koñfay-roñs*

confession la confession *koñfe-syoñ*

confirm confirmer *koñfeer-may*

congratulations félicitations! *faylee-seeta-syoñ*

connection la correspondance *kores-poñdoñs*

constipated constipé *koñstee-pay*

consulate le consulat *koñsoo-la*

contact contacter *koñtaktay*

contact lenses les verres *(mpl)* de contact *vehr duh koñtakt*

Continental breakfast le café complet *kafay koñpleh*

contraceptive le contraceptif *koñtra-septeef*

cook le cuisinier/la cuisinière *kweezee-nyay/kweezee-nyehr*

cooker la cuisinière *kweezee-nyehr*

cool frais/fraîche *freh/fresh*

copy¹ *n* la copie *kopee*

copy² *vb* copier *kopyay*

corkscrew le tire-bouchon *teer-booshoñ*

corner le coin *kwañ*

cornflakes les cornflakes *cornflakes*

cortisone la cortisone *korteezon*

cosmetics les cosmétiques *(mpl) kozmay-teek*

cost le coût *koo*

cotton le coton *kotoñ*

cotton wool le coton hydrophile *kotoñ eedro-feel*

couchette la couchette *koo-shet*

cough la toux *too*

country *(not town)* la campagne *koñpa-nyuh; (nation)* le pays *pay-ee*

couple *(two people)* le couple *koopl*

courgette la courgette *koor-zhet*

courier le guide *geed*

course *(of meal)* le plat *pla*

cover charge le couvert *koovehr*

crab le crabe *krab*

crash helmet le casque protecteur *kask protek-tur*

cream la crème *krem*

credit card la carte de crédit *kart duh kraydee*

crisps les chips *(mpl) sheeps*

croquette la croquette *kro-ket*

cross *(road)* traverser *travehrsay*

crossroads le carrefour *karfoor*

crowded bondé *boñday*

cruise la croisière *krwaz-yehr*

cucumber le concombre *koñkoñbr*

cup la tasse *tas*

cupboard le placard *plakar*

currant le raisin sec *rayzañ sek*

current le courant *kooroñ*

cushion le coussin *koossañ*

custard la crème anglaise *krem oñglez*

customs la douane *dwan*
cut[1] *n* la coupure *koopoor*
cut[2] *vb* couper *koopay*
cutlery les couverts *(mpl) koovehr*
cycle la bicyclette *bee-see-klet*
cycling le cyclisme *seeklees-muh*

daily *(each day)* tous les jours *too lay zhoor*
damage *n* les dégâts *(mpl) dayga*
damp humide *oomeed*
dance[1] *n* le bal *bal*
dance[2] *vb* danser *doñsay*
dangerous dangereux *doñ-zhuruh*
dark foncé *foñsay*
date la date *dat*
date of birth la date de naissance *dat duh neh-soñs*
daughter la fille *feey*
day le jour *zhoor*
dear cher *shehr*
decaffeinated décaféiné *daykafay-eenay*
deck chair la chaise longue *shez loñg*
declare déclarer *daykla-ray*
deep profond *profoñ*
deep freeze le congélateur *koñzhayla-tuhr*
defrost dégivrer *day-zhee-vray*
de-ice dégivrer *day-zhee-vray*
delay le retard *ruhtar*
delicious délicieux *daylee-syuh*
dentist le dentiste *doñteest*
dentures le dentier *doñ-tyay*
deodorant le déodorant *dayo-do-roñ*

department store le grand magasin *groñ maga-zañ*
departure le départ *daypar*
departure lounge la salle de départ *sal duh daypar*
deposit le dépôt *daypo*
dessert le dessert *dessehr*
details les détails *(mpl) daytye*
detergent le détergent *daytehr-zhoñ*
detour la déviation *day-vya-syoñ*
develop développer *day-vlopay*
diabetic diabétique *dya-bay-teek*
dialling code l'indicatif *(m) añdee-ka-teef*
diamond le diamant *dya-moñ*
diarrhoea la diarrhée *dya-ray*
diary l'agenda *(m) a-zhañda*
dictionary le dictionnaire *deek-syo-nehr*
diesel le gas-oil *gaz-oil*
diet le régime *ray-zheem*
different différent *deefay-roñ*
difficult difficile *deefee-seel*
dinghy le youyou *yoo-yoo*
dining room la salle à manger *sal a moñ-zhay*
dinner le dîner *deenay*
direct *(train etc)* direct *deerekt*
directory l'annuaire *(m) anwehr*
dirty sale *sal*
disabled handicapé *oñdee-kapay*
disco la discothèque *deesko-tek*
discount le rabais *rabeh*
dish le plat *pla*
dishwasher le lave-vaisselle *lav-veh-sel*
disinfectant le désinfectant *dayzañ-fek-toñ*

distilled water l'eau *(f)* distillée *oh deestee-lay*

divorced divorcé *deevor-say*

dizzy pris de vertige *pree duh vehr-tizh*

do faire *fehr*

doctor le médecin *maydsañ*

documents les papiers *(mpl)* papyay

doll la poupée *poopay*

dollar le dollar

door la porte *port*

double double *doobl*

double bed le grand lit *groñ lee*

double room la chambre pour deux personnes *shoñbr poor duh pehrson*

doughnut le beignet *bay-nyay*

down: to go down *(downstairs)* descendre *deh-soñdr*

downstairs en bas *oñ ba*

draught le courant d'air *kooroñ dehr*

dress¹ *n* la robe *rob*

dress² *vb* **: to get dressed** s'habiller *sabee-yay*

dressing *(for food)* la vinaigrette *veenay-gret*

drink¹ *n* la boisson *bwassoñ*

drink² *vb* boire *bwar*

drinking chocolate le chocolat chaud *shoko-la shoh*

drinking water l'eau *(f)* potable *oh po-tabl*

drive conduire *koñ-dweer*

driver *(of car)* le conducteur *koñdook-tur*

driving licence le permis de conduire *pehrmee duh koñdweer*

drunk ivre *eevr*

dry¹ *adj* sec/sèche *sek/sesh*

dry² *vb* sécher *sayshay*

dry-cleaner's le pressing *presseeng*

duck le canard *kanar*

dummy la sucette *soo-set*

during pendant *poñdoñ*

duty-free exempté de douane *exoñ-tay duh dwan*

duty-free shop la boutique hors taxe *booteek or tax*

duvet la couette *kwet*

dynamo la dynamo *deena-mo*

each chacun/chacune *shakuñ/ shakoon*

ear l'oreille *(f)* o-ray

earlier plus tôt *ploo toh*

early tôt *toh*

earrings les boucles *(fpl)* d'oreille *bookl do-ray*

east l'est *(m)* est

Easter Pâques *(m or fpl)* pak

easy facile *faseel*

eat manger *moñ-zhay*

eel l'anguille *(f)* oñgeey

egg l'oeuf *(m)* uf; **fried egg** l'oeuf frit *uf free*; **hard-boiled egg** l'oeuf dur *uf door*; **scrambled eggs** les oeufs brouillés *uh broo-yay*

either: either one l'un ou l'autre *luñ oo lohtr*

elastic l'élastique *(m)* aylas-teek

elastic band l'élastique *aylas-teek*

electric électrique *aylek-treek*

electrician l'électricien *(m)* aylek-tree-syañ*

electricity l'électricité *(f)* aylek-tree-seetay

electricity meter le compteur d'électricité

electric razor le rasoir électrique *razwahr aylek-treek*

embassy l'ambassade *(f)* oñba-sad

emergency: it's an emergency c'est très urgent *seh trayz oor-zhoñ*

empty vide *veed*

end la fin *fañ*

engaged *(to be married)* fiancé *fyoñ-say*; *(toilet, phone)* occupé *okoopay*

engine le moteur *mo-tur*

England l'Angleterre *(f)* oñgluh-tehr*

English anglais *oñgleh*

enjoy oneself s'amuser *samoo-say*

enough assez *assay*

enquiry desk les renseignements *(mpl)* roñseh-nyuh-moñ

entertainment les divertissements *(mpl)* deevehr-tees-moñ

entrance l'entrée *(f)* oñtray

entrance fee le prix d'entrée *pree doñtray*

envelope l'enveloppe *(f)* oñvuh-lop

equipment l'équipement *(m)* aykeep-moñ

escalator l'escalier *(m)* roulant *eska-lyay rooloñ*

especially surtout *soortoo*

essential indispensable *añdee-spoñ-sabl*

Eurocheque l'eurochèque *(m)* uhro-shek

Europe l'Europe *(f)* uhrop

evening le soir *swahr;* **in the evening** le soir

evening meal le dîner *deenay*

every chaque *shak*

everyone tout le monde *too luh moñd*

everything tout *too*

excellent excellent *ekseh-loñ*

except sauf *sohf*

excess luggage l'excédent *(m)* de bagages *eksay-doñ duh bagazh*

exchange¹ *n* l'échange *(m)* ay-shoñzh

exchange² *vb* échanger *ay-shoñ-zhay*

exchange rate le taux de change *toh duh shoñzh*

excursion l'excursion *(f)* ekskoor-syoñ

excuse: excuse me! *(sorry)* excusez-moi *eksoo-zay-mwa*

exhaust pipe le pot d'échappement *poh dayshap-moñ*

exhibition l'exposition *(f)* ekspo-zee-syoñ

exit la sortie *sortee*

expensive cher *shehr*

expert l'expert *(m)* ekspehr

expire *(ticket, passport)* expirer *ekspee-ray*

express¹ *n* *(train)* le rapide *rapeed*

express² *adj* *(parcel etc)* par exprès *par ekspress*

extra: extra money plus d'argent *ploos dar-zhoñ*

eye l'oeil *(m)* uhy

eye liner l'eye-liner *(m)* eye-liner

eye shadow l'ombre *(f)* à paupières *oñbra poh-pyehr*

face le visage *veezazh*

facilities les installations *(fpl) añsta-la-syoñ*

faint s'évanouir *sayva-nweer*

fainted évanoui *ayva-nwee*

fair *(fun fair)* la fête foraine *fet fo-ren*

fall tomber *toñbay*

family la famille *fa-meey*

famous célèbre *say-lehbr*

fan *(electric)* le ventilateur *voñtee-la-tur*

fan belt la courroie de ventilateur *koorwa duh voñtee-la-tur*

far loin *lwañ*

fare le prix du billet *pree doo bee-yay*

farm la ferme *fehrm*

fast rapide *rapeed*

fat gros *groh*

father le père *pehr*

fault: it's not my fault ce n'était pas de ma faute *suh naytay pa duh ma foht*

favourite préféré *prayfay-ray*

feed donner à manger *donay a moñ-zhay*

feel tâter *tahtay*; **I feel sick** j'ai envie de vomir *zhay oñvee duh vomeer*

ferry le ferry *fayree*

festival le festival *festee-val*

fetch aller chercher *alay shehr-shay*

fever la fièvre *fyeh-vr*

few: a few un peu (de ...) *uñ puh (duh)*

fiancé(e) le fiancé/la fiancée *fyoñ-say*

field le champ *shoñ*

fill remplir *roñpleer*; **to fill up**

(container) remplir *roñpleer*; **fill it up!** le plein! *luh plañ*

fillet le filet *fileh*

film le film *feelm*

filter le filtre *feeltr*

filter-tipped à bout filtre *a boo feeltr*

finish finir *feeneer*

fire le feu *fuh*; **fire!** au feu! *oh fuh*

fire brigade les pompiers *(mpl) poñ-pyay*

fire extinguisher l'extincteur *(m) ekstañk-tur*

firework le feu d'artifice *fuh dartee-fees*

first premier *pruhm-yay*

first aid les premiers soins *(mpl) pruhm-yay swañ*

first class en première *oñ pruhm-yehr*

first floor le premier étage *pruhm-yehr ay-tazh*

first name le prénom *praynoñ*

fish¹ *n* le poisson *pwasoñ*

fish² *vb* pêcher *pay-shay*

fit¹: it doesn't fit ça ne me va pas *sa nuh muh va pa*

fit² *n (medical)* en forme *oñ form*

fix fixer *fiksay*

fizzy pétillant *paytee-yoñ*

flash le flash

flask le thermos *tehrmos*

flat *(apartment)* l'appartement *(m) apart-moñ*

flat tyre la crevaison *kruhveh-soñ*

flight le vol *vol*

flippers les palmes *(fpl) palm*

floor *(of building)* l'étage *(m) ay-tazh*;

(of room) le plancher *ploñshay*

flour la farine *fareen*

flower la fleur *flur*

flu la grippe *greep*

fly la mouche *moosh*

fly sheet le double toit *doobl twah*

fog le brouillard *broo-yar*

follow suivre *sweevr*

food la nourriture *nooree-toor*

food poisoning l'intoxication *(f)* alimentaire *añtok-seeka-syoñ alee-moñ-tehr*

foot le pied *pyay; (measure)* see **CONVERSION CHARTS**

football le football *foot-bal*

for *(in exchange for)* pour *poor*

foreign étranger *aytroñ-zhay*

forest la forêt *foreh*

forget oublier *ooblee-ay*

fork la fourchette *foor-shet; (in road)* l'embranchement *(m) oñbroñsh-moñ*

fortnight la quinzaine *kañzen*

fountain la fontaine *foñ-ten*

France la France *froñs*

free *(not occupied)* libre *leebr; (costing nothing)* gratuit *gratwee*

freezer le congélateur *koñ-zhayla-tur*

French français *froñseh*

French beans les haricots verts *(mpl) aree-koh vehr*

frequent fréquent *fraykoñ*

fresh frais *freh*

fridge le frigo *freego*

fried frit *free*

friend l'ami/l'amie *amee*

from de *duh*

front le devant *duhvoñ*

frozen *(food)* surgelé *soor-zhuh-lay*

fruit le fruit *frwee*

fruit juice le jus de fruit *zhoo duh frwee*

fruit salad la salade de fruits *sa-lad duh frwee*

frying-pan la poêle *pwahl*

fuel le combustible *koñboo-steebl*

fuel pump la pompe d'alimentation *poñp dalee-moñta-syoñ*

full plein *plañ*

full board la pension complète *poñ-syoñ koñplet*

funny *(amusing)* amusant *amoo-zoñ*

fur la fourrure *foo-roor*

fuse le fusible *foo-zeebl*

gallery la galerie *galree*

gallon see **CONVERSION CHARTS**

gambling le jeu *zhuh*

game le jeu *zhuh*

garage le garage *garazh*

garden le jardin *zhardañ*

garlic l'ail *(m) eye*

gas le gaz *gaz*

gas cylinder la bouteille de gaz *bootay duh gaz*

gear la vitesse *vee-tess*

Geneva Genève *zhuhnev*

gentleman le monsieur *muhsyuh*

gents' les toilettes *(fpl) twalet*

genuine authentique *ohtoñ-teek*

German allemand *almoñ*

German measles la rubéole *roobay-ol*

Germany l'Allemagne *(f) alma-nyuh*

get *(obtain)* obtenir *optuh-neer;* **to get into** *(vehicle)* monter *moñtay;* **to get off** *(bus etc)* descendre *dessoñdr*

gift le cadeau *kadoh*

gift shop la boutique de souvenirs *booteek duh soov-neer*

gin le gin *djeen*

ginger le gingembre *zhañ-zhoñbr*

girl la fille *feey*

girlfriend la petite amie *puteet ami*

give donner *donay*

glass le verre *vehr*

glasses les lunettes *(fpl) loo-net*

gloves les gants *(mpl) goñ*

glucose le glucose *gloo-koz*

glue la colle *kol*

go aller *alay;* **to go back** retourner *ruhtoornay;* **to go down** *(downstairs etc)* descendre *dessoñdr;* **to go in** entrer *oñtray;* **to go out** *(leave)* sortir *sorteer*

goggles les lunettes *(fpl)* protectrices *loonet protek-trees;* *(for swimming)* les lunettes *(fpl)* de plongée *loonet duh ploñ-zhay*

gold l'or *(m) or*

golf le golf *golf*

golf course le terrain de golf *teh-rañ duh golf*

good bon/bonne *boñ/bon*

good afternoon bonjour *boñ-zhoor*

goodbye au revoir *oh ruhvwahr*

good evening bonsoir *boñswahr*

good morning bonjour *boñ-zhoor*

good night bonne nuit *bon nwee*

goose l'oie *(f) wa*

gramme le gramme *gram*

grandfather le grand-père *groñ-pehr*

grandmother la grand-mère *groñ-mehr*

grapefruit le pamplemousse *poñpluh-moos*

grapefruit juice le jus de pamplemousse *zhoo duh poñpluh-moos*

grapes les raisins *(mpl) rayzañ*

grass l'herbe *(f) ehrb*

greasy gras *gra*

green vert *vehr*

green card la carte verte *kart vehrt*

grey gris *gree*

grilled grillé *greeyay*

grocer's l'épicerie *(f) ay-pees-ree*

ground la terre *tehr*

ground floor le rez-de-chaussée *ray-duh-shoh-say*

groundsheet le tapis de sol *tapee duh sol*

group le groupe *groop*

guarantee la garantie *garoñ-tee*

guard *(on train)* le chef de train *shef duh trañ*

guest *(house guest)* l'invité(e) *(m/f) añvee-tay;* *(in hotel)* le/la client(e) *klee-oñ(t)*

guesthouse la pension *poñ-syoñ*

guide le guide *geed*

guidebook le guide *geed*

guided tour la visite guidée *veezeet geeday*

gym shoes les chaussures de tennis *shohsoor duh tenees*

haemorrhoids les hémorroïdes *(fpl)* *aymo-ro-eed*

hair les cheveux *(mpl)* *shuhvuh*

hairbrush la brosse à cheveux *bros a shuhvuh*

haircut la coupe (de cheveux) *koop duh shuhvuh*

hairdresser *(male)* le coiffeur *kwafur; (female)* la coiffeuse *kwa-fuz*

hairdryer le sèche-cheveux *sesh-shuhvuh*

hairgrip la pince à cheveux *pañs a shuhvuh*

hair spray la laque *lak*

half la moitié *mwat-yay;* **a half bottle** la demi-bouteille *duhmee-bootay*

half board la demi-pension *duhmee-poñ-syoñ*

half fare le demi-tarif *duhmee-tareef*

ham le jambon *zhoñboñ*

hand la main *mañ*

handbag le sac à main *sak a mañ*

handicapped handicapé *oñdee-kapay*

handkerchief le mouchoir *mooshwahr*

hand luggage les bagages *(mpl)* à main *bagazh a mañ*

hand-made fait main *feh mañ*

hangover la gueule de bois *gul duh bwa*

happen arriver *areevay;* **what happened?** qu'est-ce qui s'est passé? *kes kee seh passay*

happy heureux *uruh*

harbour le port *por*

hard dur *door*

hat le chapeau *shapo*

have avoir *avwar; see* **GRAMMAR**

hay fever le rhume des foins *room day fwañ*

hazelnut la noisette *nwa-zet*

he il *eel; see* **GRAMMAR**

head la tête *tet*

headache: I have a headache j'ai mal à la tête *zhay mal a la tet*

head waiter le maître d'hôtel *mehtr dotel*

hear entendre *oñtoñdr*

heart le coeur *kur*

heart attack la crise cardiaque *kreez kard-yak*

heater l'appareil *(m)* de chauffage *apa-ray duh shohfazh*

heating le chauffage *shohfazh*

heavy lourd *loor*

hello bonjour *boñ-zhoor; (on telephone)* allô *alo*

help[1] *n* l'aide *(f)* led; **help!** au secours! *oh suhkoor*

help[2] *vb* aider *ayday*

herb l'herbe *(f)* ehrb

here ici *eesee*

high haut *oh*

high blood pressure la tension *toñ-syoñ*

high chair la chaise haute *shez oht*

high tide la marée haute *maray oht*

hill la colline *koleen*

hill-walking la randonnée en montagne *roñdo-nay oñ moñta-nyuh*

hire louer *loo-ay*

hit frapper *frapay*

hitchhike faire de l'auto-stop *fehr duh lohto-stop*

hold tenir *tuhneer; (contain)* contenir *koñ-tuhneer*

hold-up *(traffic jam)* l'embouteillage *(m) oñboo-tay-yazh*

hole le trou *troo*

holiday les vacances *(fpl) vakoñs;* **on holiday** en vacances *oñ vakoñs*

home la maison *mehzoñ*

homesick: to be homesick avoir le mal du pays *avwar luh mal doo pay-ee*

honey le miel *myel*

honeymoon la lune de miel *loon duh myel*

hope espérer *espay-ray;* **I hope so/not** j'espère que oui/non *zheh-spehr k'wee/kuh noñ*

hors d'oeuvre le hors d'oeuvre *or duhv-ruh*

horse le cheval *shuh-val*

hose la durit *dooreet*

hospital l'hôpital *(m) opee-tal*

hot chaud *shoh;* **I'm hot** j'ai chaud *zhay shoh;* **it's hot** *(weather)* il fait chaud *eel feh shoh*

hotel l'hôtel *(m) ohtel*

hour l'heure *(f) ur*

house la maison *mehzoñ*

house wine la réserve du patron *ray-zehrv doo patroñ*

hovercraft l'aéroglisseur *(m) a-ehro-glee-sur*

how *(in what way)* comment *komoñ;* **how much?/how many?** combien? *koñ-byañ;* **how are you?** comment allez-vous? *komoñ talay voo*

hungry: I am hungry j'ai faim *zhay fañ*

hurry: I'm in a hurry je suis pressé *zhuh swee pressay*

hurt: my back hurts j'ai mal au dos *zhay mal oh doh*

husband le mari *maree*

hydrofoil l'hydrofoil *(m) eedro-foil*

I je *zhuh;* see **GRAMMAR**

ice la glace *glas*

ice cream la glace *glas*

iced glacé *glassay*

ice lolly le bâtonnet glacé *bahtonnay glassay*

ice rink la patinoire *pateen-wahr*

if si *see*

ignition l'allumage *(m) aloo-mazh*

ill malade *malad*

immediately immédiatement *eemay-dyat-moñ*

important important *añpor-toñ*

impossible impossible *añpo-seebl*

in dans *doñ*

inch see **CONVERSION CHARTS**

included compris *koñpree*

indigestion l'indigestion *(f) añdee-zhes-tyoñ*

indoors à l'intérieur *a lañtay-ryur*

infectious infectieux *añfek-suh*

information les renseignements *(mpl) roñsay-nyuh-moñ*

information office le bureau de renseignements *booroh duh roñsay-nyuh-moñ*

injection la piqûre *peekoor*

injured blessé *blessay*

ink l'encre *(f) oñkr*

insect l'insecte *(m) añsekt*

insect bite la piqûre (d'insecte)

peekoor (dañsekt)

insect repellent la crème anti-insecte *krem oñtee-añsekt*

inside l'intérieur *(m) añtay-ryur*; **inside the car** dans la voiture *doñ la vwatoor*

instant coffee le café instantané *kafay añstoñ-ta-nay*

instead of au lieu de *oh lyuh duh*

instructor le moniteur *monee-tur*

insulin l'insuline *(f) añsoo-leen*

insurance l'assurance *(f) asoo-roñs*

insurance certificate la carte d'assurance *(f) kart dasoo-roñs*

interesting intéressant *añtay-reh-soñ*

international international *añtehr-na-syo-nal*

interpreter l'interprète *(m/f) añtehr-pret*

into dans *doñ*

invitation l'invitation *(f) añvee-ta-syoñ*

invite inviter *añvee-tay*

invoice la facture *fak-toor*

Ireland l'Irlande *(f) eer-loñd*

Irish irlandais *eerloñ-deh*

iron *(for clothes)* le fer *fehr*

ironmonger's la quincaillerie *kañkye-yuhree*

is *see* **GRAMMAR**

island l'île *(f) eel*

it il/elle *eel/elle; see* **GRAMMAR**

Italian italien *eeta-lyañ*

Italy l'Italie *(f) eeta-lee*

itch la démangeaison *daymoñ-zheh-zoñ*

jack *(for car)* le cric *kreek*

jacket la veste *vest*

jam *(food)* la confiture *koñfee-toor*

jammed coincé *kwañ-say*

jar *(container)* le pot *poh*

jazz le jazz *jaz*

jeans le jean *jeen*

jelly *(dessert)* la gelée *zhuhlay*

jellyfish la méduse *maydooz*

jeweller's la bijouterie *beezhoo-tree*

jewellery les bijoux *(mpl) beezhoo*

Jewish juif *zhweef*

job le travail *tra-vye*

jog: to go jogging faire du jogging *fehr doo jogging*

joke la plaisanterie *playzoñ-tree*

journey le voyage *vwa-yazh*

jug le pot *poh*

juice le jus *zhoo*

jump leads les câbles *(mpl)* de raccordement de batterie *kabl duh rakord-moñ duh batree*

junction *(road)* la bifurcation *beefoorka-syoñ*

just: just two deux seulement *duh sulmoñ*; **I've just arrived** je viens d'arriver *zhuh vyañ daree-vay*

keep *(retain)* garder *garday*

kettle la bouilloire *booy-wahr*

key le clé *klay*

kidneys *(as food)* les rognons *(mpl) ro-nyoñ*

kilo le kilo *keeloh*

kilometre le kilomètre *keeloh-metr*

kind[1] *n (sort, type)* la sorte *sort*

kind[2] *adj (person)* gentil *zhoñ-teey*

kiss embrasser *oñbrassay*

kitchen la cuisine *kweezeen*

knife le couteau *kootoh*

know *(facts)* savoir *sav-wahr;* *(be acquainted with)* connaître *koneh-tr*

lace la dentelle *doñtel*

ladder l'échelle *(f)* ayshel

ladies' les toilettes *(fpl)* twalet

lady la dame *dam*

lager la bière blonde *bee-ayr bloñd*

lake le lac *lak*

lamb l'agneau *(m)* a-nyoh

lamp la lampe *loñp*

lane la ruelle *rooel;* *(of motorway)* la voie *vwa*

language la langue *loñg*

large grand *groñ*

last dernier *dehr-nyay;* **last week** la semaine dernière *smen dehr-nyehr*

late tard *tar;* **the train is late** le train a du rétard *trañ a doo ruhtar*

later plus tard *ploo tar*

launderette la laverie automatique *lavree ohtohma-teek*

laundry service le service de blanchisserie *sehrvees duh bloñshees-ree*

lavatory les toilettes *(fpl)* twalet

lawyer l'avocat *(m)* avo-ka

laxative le laxatif *laksa-teef*

layby l'aire *(f)* de stationnement *ehr duh sta-syon-moñ*

lead *(electric)* le fil *feel*

leader *(of group)* le chef de groupe *shef duh groop*

leak *(of gas, liquid)* la fuite *fweet;* *(in roof)* la fuite *fweet*

learn apprendre *aproñdr*

least: at least au moins *mwañ*

leather le cuir *kweer*

leave partir *parteer;* *(leave behind)* laisser *lay-say*

leeks les poireaux *(mpl)* pwaro

left: (on/to the) left à gauche *a gohsh*

left-luggage (office) la consigne *koñsee-nyuh*

leg la jambe *zhoñb*

lemon le citron *seetroñ*

lemonade la limonade *leemo-nad*

lemon tea le thé au citron *tay oh seetroñ*

lend prêter *pretay*

lens l'objectif *(m)* ob-zhek-teef

less (than) moins (de) *mwañ (duh)*

lesson la leçon *luhsoñ*

let *(allow)* permettre *pehrmetr;* *(hire out)* louer *looay*

letter la lettre *letr*

lettuce la laitue *laytoo*

library la bibliothèque *beebleeo-tek*

licence le permis *pehrmee*

lid le couvercle *koovehr-kl*

lie down se coucher *suh kooshay*

lifeboat le canot de sauvetage *kano duh sohvtazh*

lifeguard le surveillant de plage *soorvay-yoñ duh plazh*

life jacket le gilet de sauvetage *zheeleh duh sohvtazh*

lift l'ascenseur *(m)* asoñ-sur

lift pass *(on ski slopes)* l'abonnement *(m)* aux remontées *abon-moñ oh ruhmoñ-tay*

light la lumière *loo-myehr*; **have you got a light?** avez-vous du feu? *avay-voo doo fuh*

light bulb l'ampoule (f) *oñpool*

lighter le briquet *breekay*

like¹ *prep* comme *com*; **like this** comme ça *com sa*

like² *vb* aimer *aymay*; **I like coffee** j'aime le café *zhem luh kafay*

lime *(fruit)* la lime *leem*

line la ligne *leen-yuh*

lip salve la pommade pour les lèvres *pomad poor lay lehvr*

lipstick le rouge à lèvres *roozh a lehvr*

liqueur la liqueur *lee-kur*

listen (to) écouter *aykootay*

litre le litre *leetr*

little: a little milk un peu de lait *uñ puh d'leh*

live vivre *veevr*; **I live in London** j'habite (à) Londres *zhabeet-(a) loñdr*

liver le foie *fwa*

living room la salle de séjour *sal duh say-zhoor*

loaf le pain *pañ*

lobster le homard *omar*

local *(wine, speciality)* local *lokal*

lock¹ *vb (door)* fermer a clé *fehrmay a klay*

lock² *n (on door, box)* la serrure *sehroor*

lollipop la sucette *soosett*

London Londres *loñdr*

long long *loñ*; **for a long time** longtemps *loñtoñ*

look regarder *ruhgar-day*; **to look after** garder *garday*; **to look for** chercher *shehr-shay*

lorry le camion *kamyoñ*

lose perdre *pehrdr*

lost *(object)* perdu *pehrdoo*; **I have lost ...** j'ai perdu ... *zhay pehrdoo*

lost property office le bureau des objets trouvés *booroh dayz ob-zhay troovay*

lot: a lot beaucoup *bohkoo*

lotion la lotion *losyoñ*

loud fort *for*

lounge *(in hotel)* le salon *saloñ*

love *(person)* aimer *aymay*; **I love swimming** j'aime nager *zhem nazhay*

lovely charmant *sharmoñ*

low bas *ba*

low tide la marée basse *ma-ray bas*

luggage les bagages *(mpl) bagazh*

luggage allowance le poids maximum autorisé *pwah maksee-mom oto-reezay*

luggage rack *(on car, in train)* le porte-bagages *port-bagazh*

luggage tag l'étiquette *(f)* à bagages *aytee-ket a bagazh*

luggage trolley le chariot (à bagages) *sharee-o (a bagazh)*

lunch le déjeuner *day-zhuh-nay*

Luxembourg Luxembourg *(m) looksoñ-boor*

luxury de luxe *duh loox*

macaroni les macaronis *(mpl) makaro-nee*

machine la machine *masheen*

madam madame *madam*

magazine la revue *ruhvoo*

maid la domestique *domes-teek*

main principal *prañsee-pal*

main course le plat de résistance *pla duh rayzee-stoñs*

mains (electric) le secteur *sek-tur*

make faire *fehr*

make-up le maquillage *makee-yazh*

mallet le maillet *mye-yay*

man l'homme *om*

manager le directeur *deerek-tur*

many beaucoup *bohkoo*

map la carte *kart*

margarine la margarine *marga-reen*

market le marché *marshay*

marmalade la confiture d'oranges *koñfeetoor do-roñzh*

married marié *mar-yay*

marzipan la pâte d'amandes *paht damoñd*

mascara le mascara *maska-ra*

mass (in church) la messe *mes*

match l'allumette (f) *aloo-met*

material (cloth) le tissu *teesoo*

matter: it doesn't matter ça ne fait rien *sa nuh feh ryañ*; **what's the matter?** qu'est-ce qu'il y a? *keskeel-ya*

mayonnaise la mayonnaise *ma-yonez*

meal le repas *ruhpa*

mean (signify) signifier *see-nyee-fyay*; **what does this mean?** qu'est-ce que cela signifie? *keskuh seh-la see-nyee-fee*

measles la rougeole *roo-zhol*

meat la viande *vyoñd*

mechanic le mécanicien *mayka-nee-syañ*

medicine le médicament *maydee-ka-moñ*

medium à point *a pwañ*

meet rencontrer *roñkoñ-tray*

melon le melon *muh-loñ*

melt fondre *foñdr*

member (of club etc) le membre *moñbr*

menu le menu *muhnoo*

meringue la meringue *muh-rañg*

message le message *messazh*

metal le métal *maytal*

meter le compteur *koñtur*

metre le mètre *metr*

migraine la migraine *meegren*

mile see **CONVERSION CHARTS**

milk le lait *leh*

milkshake le milk-shake

millimetre le millimètre *meelee-metr*

million le million *meel-yoñ*

mince le bifteck haché *beeftek ashay*

mind: do you mind if I...? est-ce que cela vous gêne si ...? *eskuh sla voo zhen see*

mineral water l'eau (f) minérale *oh meenay-ral*

minimum le minimum *meenee-mum*

minister (church) le pasteur *pastur*

minor road la route secondaire *root suhgoñ-dehr*

mint (herb) la menthe *moñt*; (sweet) le bonbon à la menthe *boñboñ a la moñt*

minute la minute *meenoot*

mirror la glace *glass*

miss *(train etc)* manquer *moñkay*

Miss mademoiselle *mad-mwa-zel*

missing disparu *deespa-roo*

mistake l'erreur *(f) eh-rur*

misty brumeux *broomuh*

misunderstanding: there's been a misunderstanding il y a eu une méprise *eel ya oo oon may-preez*

modern moderne *modehrn*

moisturizer le lait hydratant *leh eedra-toñ*

monastery le monastère *mona-stehr*

money l'argent *(m) ar-zhoñ*

money order le mandat *moñ-da*

month le mois *mwa*

monument le monument *monoo-moñ*

mop *(for floor)* le balai à laver *balay a lavay*

more (than) plus (de) *ploos (duh)*; **more wine** plus de vin *ploo duh vañ*

morning le matin *matañ*

mosquito le moustique *moo-steek*

most le plus *ploos*

mother la mère *mehr*

motor le moteur *mo-tur*

motor boat le bateau à moteur *batoh a mo-tur*

motor cycle la moto *moto*

motorway l'autoroute *(f) ohto-root*

mountain la montagne *moñ-tanyuh*

mousse la mousse *moos*

mouth la bouche *boosh*

move bouger *boo-zhay*

Mr Monsieur *muhsyuh*

Mrs, Ms Madame *madam*

much beaucoup *bohkoo*; **too much** trop *troh*

mumps les oreillons *(mpl) oray-yoñ*

museum le musée *moozay*

mushroom le champignon *shoñpee-nyoñ*

music la musique *moo-zeek*

mussel la moule *mool*

must: I must je dois *zhuh dwa*; **he must** il doit *eel dwa*

mustard la moutarde *mootard*

mutton le mouton *mootoñ*

nail *(metal)* le clou *kloo*; *(finger)* l'ongle *(m) oñgl*

nail polish le vernis à ongles *vehrnee a oñgl*

nail polish remover le dissolvant *dee-sol-voñ*

naked nu *noo*

name le nom *noñ*

napkin la serviette *sehr-vyet*

nappy la couche *koosh*

narrow étroit *ay-trwa*

nationality la nationalité *na-syonalee-tay*

navy blue bleu marine *bluh mareen*

near près *preh*; **near the bank** près de la banque *preh duh la boñk*

necessary nécessaire *nayseh-sehr*

neck le cou *koo*

necklace le collier *ko-lyay*

need: I need ... j'ai besoin de ... *zhay buh-zwañ duh ...*

needle l'aiguille *(f) aygwee*

negative *(photography)* le négatif *nayga-teef*

neighbour le voisin *vwa-zañ*

never jamais *zhamay*; **I never drink wine** je ne bois jamais le vin *zhuh nuh bwa zhamay luh vañ*

new nouveau/nouvelle *noovo/noovel*

news la nouvelle *noovel*

newsagent le marchand de journaux *marshoñ duh zhoorno*

newspaper le journal *zhoor-nal*

New Year le Nouvel An *noovel oñ*

New Zealand la Nouvelle-Zélande *noovel zayloñd*

next: the next train le prochain train *proshañ tran*; **next week** la semaine prochaine *smen proshen*

nice bien *byañ*

night la nuit *nwee*

night club la boîte de nuit *bwat duh nwee*

nightdress la chemise de nuit *shuhmeez duh nwee*

no non *noñ*; **no thank you** non merci *noñ mehrsee*

nobody personne *pehrson*

noisy bruyant *brwee-yoñ*

non-alcoholic non alcoolisé *noñ alko-lee-zay*

none aucun(e) *ohkuñ/ohkoon*; **there's none left** il n'en reste plus *eel noñ rest ploo*

non-smoking *(compartment)* non-fumeur *noñ-foomur*

north le nord *nor*

Northern Ireland l'Irlande *(f)* du Nord *eerloñd doo nor*

not pas *pa*; **I am not ...** je ne suis pas ... *zhuh nuh swee pa ...*

note *(bank note)* le billet *bee-yay*; *(letter)* le billet *bee-yay*

note pad le bloc-notes *blok-not*

nothing rien *ryañ*

now maintenant *mañt-noñ*

number le nombre *noñbr*

nurse l'infirmière *(f)* añ-feerm-yehr

nursery slope la piste pour débutants *peest poor dayboo-toñ*

nut *(to eat)* la noix *nwa*; *(for bolt)* l'écrou *aykroo*

occasionally de temps en temps *duh toñz oñ toñ*

of de *duh*

off *(light)* éteint *aytañ*; *(rotten)* mauvais *mohveh*

offer offrir *ofreer*

office le bureau *booroh*

often souvent *soovoñ*

oil l'huile *(f)* weel

oil filter le filtre à huile *feeltr a weel*

ointment la pommade *pomad*

O.K. bien *byañ*

old vieux/vieille *vyuh/vyay*; **how old are you?** quel âge avez-vous? *kel ahzh avay-voo*

olive oil l'huile *(f)* d'olive *weel doleev*

olives les olives *(f)* oleev

omelette l'omelette *(f)* omlet

on *(light)* allumé *aloomay*; *(engine etc)* en marche *oñ marsh*; **on (the table)** sur (la table) *soor (la tabl)*

once une fois *oon fwa*

one un/une *uñ/oon*

one-way *(street)* à sens unique *a soñs ooneek*

onion l'oignon *(m) o-nyoñ*
only seulement *sulmoñ*
open¹ *adj* ouvert *oovehr*
open² *vb* ouvrir *oov-reer*
opera l'opéra *(m) opayra*
operator le/la téléphoniste *taylay-foneest*
opposite: opposite the hotel en face de l'hôtel *oñ fas duh lohtel*
or ou *oo*
orange¹ *adj* orange *oroñzh*
orange² *n* l'orange *(f) oroñzh*
orange juice le jus d'orange *zhoo doroñzh*
order commander *komoñday*
original original *oree-zhee-nal*
other autre *ohtr*
ounce *see* CONVERSION CHARTS
out *(light)* éteint *aytañ*; **she's out** elle est sortie *el eh sortee*
outdoor *(pool etc)* en plein air *oñ plen ehr*
outside à l'extérieur *a lekstay-ree-uhr*
oven le four *foor*
over *(on top of)* au-dessus de *oh duhsoo duh*
overcharge faire payer trop cher *fehr pay-yay troh shehr*
overnight *(travel)* de nuit *duh nwee*
owe; **you owe me ...** vous me devez ... *voo muh duhvay ...*
owner le/la propriétaire *propree-ay-tehr*
oyster l'huître *(f) weetr*

pack *(luggage)* emballer *oñba-lay*

package le paquet *pakay*
package tour le voyage organisé *vwa-yazh organee-zay*
packed lunch le panier repas *panyay-ruhpa*
packet le paquet *pakay*
paddling pool le petit bain pour enfants *puhtee bañ poor oñfoñ*
paid payé *payay*
painful douloureux *dooloo-ruh*
painkiller le calmant *kalmoñ*
painting le tableau *tabloh*
pair la paire *pehr*
palace le palais *paleh*
pan la casserole *kas-rol*
pancake la crêpe *krep*
pants le slip *sleep*
paper le papier *papyay*
paraffin le pétrole *paytrol*
parcel le colis *kolee*
pardon *(I didn't understand)* comment? *komoñ*; **I beg your pardon!** pardon *pardoñ*
parent le parent *paroñ*
Paris Paris *paree*
park¹ *n* le parc *park*
park² *vb* stationner *sta-syonay*
parking disc le disque de stationnement *deesk duh sta-syon-moñ*
parsley le persil *perseey*
part la partie *partee*
party *(group)* le groupe *groop*
passenger le passager *passa-zhay*
passport le passeport *paspor*
passport control le contrôle des passeports *koñtrohl day paspor*

pasta les pâtes *(fpl)* paht
pastry la pâte *paht;* *(cake)* la pâtisserie *patees-ree*
pâté le pâté *pahtay*
path le chemin *shuh-mañ*
pay payer *pay-yay*
payment le paiement *paymoñ*
peach la pêche *pesh*
peanut la cacahuète *kaka-wet*
pear la poire *pwahr*
peas les petits pois *puhtee pwa*
peel *(fruit)* peler *puhlay*
peg *(for clothes)* la pince *pañs;* *(for tent)* la cheville *shuhveey*
pen le stylo *steelo*
pencil le crayon *kray-oñ*
penicillin la pénicilline *paynee-seeleen*
penknife le canif *kaneef*
pensioner le retraité/la retraitée *ruhtreh-tay*
pepper *(spice)* le poivre *pwavr;* *(vegetable)* le poivron *pwavroñ*
per: per hour à l'heure *a lur*
perfect parfait *parfeh*
performance la représentation *ruhpray-zoñta-syoñ*
perfume le parfum *parfuñ*
perhaps peut-être *puh-tetr*
period *(menstruation)* les règles *(fpl)* reh-gluh
perm la permanente *pehrma-noñt*
permit le permis *pehrmee*
person la personne *pehr-son*
petrol l'essence *(f)* essoñs
petrol station la station-service *sta-syoñ sehrvees*
phone *see* **telephone**

photocopy photocopier *fohtoh-kopyay*
photograph la photo *fohtoh*
picnic le pique-nique *peek-neek*
picture *(painting)* le tableau *tabloh;* *(photo)* le tableau *tabloh*
pie la tourte *toort*
piece le morceau *morsoh*
pill la pilule *peelool*
pillow l'oreiller *(m)* oray-yay
pillowcase la taie d'oreiller *tay doray-yay*
pin l'épingle *(f)* ay-pañgl
pineapple l'ananas *(m)* ana-na
pink rose *rohz*
pint *see* **CONVERSION CHARTS; a pint of ...** un demi-litre de ... *uñ duhmee leetr duh ...*
pipe la pipe *peep*
plane l'avion *(m)* a-vyoñ
plaster *(sticking plaster)* le sparadrap *spara-dra*
plastic le plastique *pla-steek*
plate l'assiette *(f)* a-syet
platform le quai *kay*
play *(games)* jouer *zhoo-ay*
playroom la salle de jeux *sal duh zhuh*
please s'il vous plaît *seel voo pleh*
pleased content *koñtoñ*
pliers la pince *pañs*
plug *(electrical)* la prise *preez*
plum la prune *proon*
plumber le plombier *ploñ-byay*
points *(in car)* les vis *(fpl)* platinées *vees platee-nay*
police la police *polees*
policeman l'agent *(m)* de police *a-*

zhoñ duh polees

police station le commissariat (de police) *komee-saree-a (duh polees)*

polish *(for shoes)* le cirage *seerazh*

polluted pollué *poloo-ay*

pony-trekking la randonnée à cheval *roñdo-nay a shuhval*

pool *(swimming)* la piscine *peeseen*

popular populaire *popoo-lehr*

pork le porc *por*

port *(seaport)* le port *por;* *(wine)* le porto *portoh*

porter *(in hotel)* le porteur *por-tur*

possible possible *po-seebl*

post mettre à la poste *metra la post*

postbox la boîte aux lettres *bwat oh letr*

postcard la carte postale *kart pos-tal*

postcode le code postal *cod pos-tal*

post office le bureau de poste *booroh duh post*

pot *(for cooking)* le pot *poh*

potato la pomme de terre *pom duh tehr*

pottery la poterie *potree*

pound la livre *leevr;* *(weight)* see **CONVERSION CHARTS**

powdered milk le lait en pudre *leh oñ poodr*

pram la voiture d'enfant *vwatoor doñfoñ*

prawn la crevette *kruh-vet*

prefer préférer *prayfay-ray*

pregnant enceinte *oñsañt*

prepare préparer *praypa-ray*

prescription l'ordonnance *(f)* ordo-*noñs*

present *(gift)* le cadeau *kadoh*

pretty joli *zholee*

price le prix *pree*

price list le tarif *tareef*

priest le prêtre *pretr*

print *(photo)* l'épreuve *(f)* aypruv*

private privé *preevay*

probably probablement *proba-bluh-moñ*

problem le problème *pro-blem*

programme le programme *program*

pronounce prononcer *pronoñ-say;* **how do you pronounce it?** comment ça se prononce? *komoñ sa suh pronoñs*

Protestant protestant *protes-toñ*

prune le pruneau *proono*

public public *poobleek*

public holiday le jour férié *zhoor fayree-ay*

pudding le dessert *dessehr*

pull tirer *teeray*

pullover le pull *pool*

puncture la crevaison *kruhveh-zoñ*

purple violet *vee-olay*

purse le porte-monnaie *port-monay*

push pousser *poosay*

put *(insert)* mettre *metr;* *(put down)* déposer *daypoh-zay*

pyjamas le pyjama *peezha-ma*

the Pyrenees les Pyrénées *(fpl)* *peeraynay*

queue la queue *kuh*

quick rapide *rapeed*

quickly vite *veet*

quiet *(place)* tranquille *troñkeel*

quilt l'édredon *(m)* aydruh-doñ*

quite (rather) assez assay;
(completely) complètement
koñplet-moñ

rabbit le lapin lapañ
racket la raquette raket
radio la radio radyo
radish le radis radee
railway station la gare gar
rain la pluie plwee
raincoat l'imperméable (m) añpehr-may-abl
raining: it's raining il pleut pluh
raisin le raisin sec rayzañ sek
rare (unique) rare rar; (steak)
saignant say-nyoñ
raspberries les framboises (fpl)
froñbwaz
rate le taux toh; **rate of exchange** le
taux de change toh duh shoñzh
raw cru kroo
razor le rasoir razwahr
razor blades les lames (fpl) de
rasoir lam duh razwahr
ready prêt preh
real vrai vray
receipt le reçu ruhsoo
recently récemment rays-moñ
reception (desk) la réception
raysep-syoñ
recipe la recette ruh-set
recommend recommander ruhko-moñday
record (music etc) le disque deesk
red rouge roozh
reduction la réduction raydook-syoñ
refill la recharge ruhsharzh

refund le remboursement roñboors-moñ
registered recommandé ruhko-moñ-day
regulation le règlement raygluh-moñ
reimburse rembourser roñboor-say
relation (family) le parent paroñ
relax se détendre suh day-toñdr
reliable (company, service) sérieux
sayree-uh
remain rester restay
remember se rappeler suh rapuh-lay
rent louer loo-ay
rental la location loka-syoñ
repair réparer raypa-ray
repeat répéter raypay-tay
reservation la réservation rayzehr-va-syoñ
reserve réserver rayzehr-vay
reserved réservé rayzehr-vay
rest[1] n (repose) le repos ruhpoh; **the
rest of the wine** le rest du vin luh
rest doo vañ
rest[2] vb se reposer suh ruhpoh-zay
restaurant le restaurant resto-roñ
restaurant car le wagon-restaurant
vagoñ-resto-roñ
return (go back) retourner
ruhtoornay; (give back) rendre roñdr
return ticket le billet aller et retour
bee-yay alay ay ruhtoor
reverse charge call l'appel (m) en
P.C.V. apel oñ pay-say-vay
rheumatism le rhumatisme rooma-teez-muh
rhubarb la rhubarbe roobarb
rice le riz ree

riding l'équitation (f) aykeeta-syoñ;
to go riding faire du cheval fehr doo
shuhval

right¹ adj (correct) exact egzakt

right² adv : **(on/to the) right** à droite
a drwat

ring la bague bag

ripe mûr moor

river la rivière ree-vyehr

the Riviera la Côte d'Azur koht da-
zoor

road la route root

road map la carte routière kart roo-
tyehr

roast rôti rohtee

roll (bread) le petit pain puhtee pañ

roof le toit twa

roof-rack la galerie gal-ree

room (in house, hotel) la pièce pyes;
(space) la place plas

room service le service des
chambres sehrvees day shoñbr

rope la corde kord

rough (sea) rugueux rooguh

round rond roñ; **round the corner**
après le coin apray le kwañ

route la route root

rowing boat le canot à rames kano
a ram

rubber le caoutchouc ka-oot-shoo

rubber band l'élastique (m) ayla-
steek

rubbish les ordures (fpl) or-door

rucksack le sac à dos sak a doh

ruins les ruines (f) rween

rum le rhum rom

run (skiing) la piste peest

rush hour les heures (fpl)
d'affluence ur dafloo-oñs

safe¹ n le coffre-fort kofr-for

safe² adj (beach, medicine) sans
danger soñ doñ-zhay

safety pin l'épingle (f) de sûreté ay-
pañgl duh soortay

sail la voile vwal

sailboard la planche à voile ploñsh
a vwal

sailing (sport) la voile vwal

salad la salade sa-lad

salad dressing la vinaigrette
veenay-gret

salmon le saumon sohmoñ

salt le sel sel

same même mem

sand le sable sabl

sandals les sandales (fpl) soñdal

sandwich le sandwich soñdweech

sanitary towel la serviette
hygiénique sehr-vyet ee-zhay-neek

sardine la sardine sardeen

sauce la sauce sohs

saucepan la casserole kas-rol

saucer la soucoupe sookoop

sauna le sauna sohna

sausage la saucisse sohsees

savoury (not sweet) salé salay

say dire deer

scallop la coquille Saint-Jacques
kokeey sañ-zhak

scarf l'écharpe (f) aysharp

school l'école (f) aykol

scissors les ciseaux (mpl) seezoh

Scotland l'Écosse (f) aykos

Scottish écossais *ayko-seh*

screw la vis *vees*

screwdriver le tournevis *toornvees*

sculpture *(object)* la sculpture *skoolptoor*

sea la mer *mehr*

seafood les fruits *(mpl)* de mer *frwee duh mehr*

seasickness le mal de mer *mal duh mehr*

seaside: at the seaside au bord de la mer *oh bor duh la mehr*

season ticket l'abonnement *(m)* *abon-moñ*

seat *(chair)* le siège *syezh; (in train, theatre)* la place *plas*

second second *suhgoñ*

second class en deuxième *oñ duh-zyem*

see voir *vwahr*

self-service le libre-service *leebr-sehrvees*

sell vendre *voñdr*

Sellotape ® le scotch *scotch*

send envoyer *oñvwa-yay*

senior citizen le retraité/la retraitée *ruhtreh-tay*

separate séparé *sayparay*

serious grave *grav*

serve servir *sehrveer*

service *(in restaurant)* le service *sehrvees*

service charge le service *sehrvees*

set menu le menu *muhnoo*

shade l'ombre *(f)* *oñbruh*

shallow peu profond *puh profoñ*

shampoo le shampooing *shoñpwañ*

shampoo and set le shampooing et mise en plis *shoñpwañ ay meezoñ-plee*

shandy le panaché *pana-shay*

share partager *parta-zhay*

shave se raser *suh razay*

shaving cream la crème à raser *krem a razay*

she elle *el; see* **GRAMMAR**

sheet le drap *dra*

shellfish le crustacé *kroosta-say*

sherry le sherry *shehree*

ship le navire *naveer*

shirt la chemise *shuhmeez*

shock absorber l'amortisseur *(m)* *amor-tee-sur*

shoe la chaussure *shoh-soor*

shop le magasin *maga-zañ*

shopping: to go shopping faire des courses *fehr day koors*

short court *koor*

short cut le raccourci *rakoor-see*

shorts le short *short*

show¹ *n* le spectacle *spek-takluh*

show² *vb* montrer *moñtray*

shower la douche *doosh*

shrimp la crevette grise *kruh-vet greez*

sick *(ill)* malade *malad*

sightseeing le tourisme *tooreez-muh*

sign le panneau *panoh*

signature la signature *seenya-toor*

silk la soie *swa*

silver argenté *ar-zhoñtay*

similar semblable *soñ-blabl*

simple simple *sañpl*

single *(unmarried)* célibataire *sayleeba-tehr; (not double)* simple sañpl; (bed, room) pour une personne poor oon pehr-son

sink l'évier (m) ay-vyay

sir Monsieur muhsyuh

sister la soeur sur

sit s'asseoir saswahr; **please sit down** asseyez-vous, je vous en prie assay-yay-voo zhuh voozoñ pree

size la taille tye

skate le patin patañ

skating (ice) le patinage patee-nazh; (roller) le skating skating

ski[1] vb faire du ski fehr doo skee

ski[2] n le ski skee

ski boots les chaussures (fpl) de ski shohsoor duh skee

skiing le ski skee

skimmed milk le lait écrémé leh aykraymay

skin la peau poh

skin diving la plongée sous-marine ploñ-zhay sooma-reen

ski pants le fuseau foozo

ski pass see **lift pass**

ski pole le bâton (de ski) bahtoñ (duh skee)

skirt la jupe zhoop

ski run la piste peest

ski suit la combinaison de ski koñbee-nezoñ

sledge la luge loozh

sleep dormir dormeer

sleeping bag le sac de couchage sak duh kooshazh

sleeping car la voiture-lit vwatoor-lee

sleeping pill le somnifère somnee-fehr

slice la tranche troñsh

slide (photograph) la diapositive dyapo-zee-teev

slipper la pantoufle poñ-toofl

slow lent loñ

small petit puhtee

smaller (than) plus petit (que) ploo puhtee (kuh)

smell l'odeur (f) o-dur

smoke[1] n la fumée foomay

smoke[2] vb fumer foomay

smoked fumé foomay

snack bar le snack snack

snorkel le tuba tooba

snow la neige nezh

snowed up enneigé oñ-neh-zhay

snowing: it's snowing il neige eel nezh

so: so much tant toñ

soap le savon savoñ

soap powder la lessive leseev

socket la prise de courant preez duh kooroñ

sock la chaussette shoh-set

soda l'eau (f) de Seltz oh duh selts

soft doux/douce doo/doos

soft drink la boisson non alcoolisée bwahsoñ noñ alko-leezay

some quelques kelkuh

someone quelqu'un kelkuñ

something quelque chose kelkuh shohz

sometimes quelquefois kelkuh-fwa

son le fils fees

song la chanson shoñsoñ

soon bientôt byañto

sore douloureux dooloo-ruh

sorry: I'm sorry! excusez-moi *exkoozay-mwa*

sort: what sort of cheese? quelle sorte de fromage? *kel sort duh fromazh*

soup le potage *potazh*

south le sud *sood*

souvenir le souvenir *soov-neer*

space la place *plas*

spade la pelle *pel*

Spain l'Espagne *(f) espanyuh*

Spanish espagnol *espa-nyol*

spanner la clé *klay*

spare wheel la roue de rechange *roo duh ruh-shoñzh*

spark plug la bougie *boo-zhee*

sparkling mousseux *moosuh*

speak parler *parlay*

special spécial *spay-syal*

speciality la spécialité *spay-syalee-tay*

speed la vitesse *vee-tes*

speed limit la limitation de vitesse *leemeeta-syoñ duh vee-tes*

spell: how do you spell it? comment ça s'écrit? *komoñ sa saykree*

spicy épicé *aypee-say*

spinach les épinards *(mpl) aypee-nard*

spirits les spiritueux *(mpl) speeree-too-uh*

sponge l'éponge *(f) aypoñzh*

spoon la cuiller *kwee-yehr*

sport le sport *spor*

spring (season) le printemps *prañtoñ*

square (in town) la place *plas*

squash (game) le squash *skwosh*; (drink) la citronnade/l'orangeade

seetro-nad/oroñzh-ad

stain la tache *tash*

stairs l'escalier *(m) eska-lyay*

stalls (theatre) l'orchestre *(m) orkestr*

stamp le timbre *tañbr*

start commencer *komoñ-say*

starter (in meal) le hors d'oeuvre or duhvr; (in car) le démarreur *dayma-rur*

station la gare *gar*

stationer's la papeterie *paptree*

stay (remain) rester *restay*; **I'm staying at the hotel ...** je suis à l'hôtel ... *zhuh sweez a lohtel ...*

steak le bifteck *beeftek*

steep raide *red*

sterling le sterling *stehrling*

stew le ragoût *ragoo*

steward le steward *steward*

stewardess l'hôtesse *(f) ohtess*

sticking plaster le sparadrap *spara-dra*

still (motionless) immobile *eemobeel*

sting la piqûre *peekoor*

stockings les bas *(mpl) ba*

stomach l'estomac *(m) esto-ma*

stomach upset l'estomac *(m)* dérangé *esto-ma dayroñ-zhay*

stop arrêter *areh-tay*

stopover la halte *alt*

storm l'orage *(m) orazh*

straight on tout droit *too drwa*

straw (for drinking) la paille *pye*

strawberry la fraise *frez*

street la rue *roo*

street map le plan des rues *ploñ day roo*

string la ficelle *fee-sel*

striped rayé *rayay*

strong fort *for*

stuck bloqué *blokay*

student *(male)* l'étudiant *aytoo-dyoñ*; *(female)* l'étudiante *aytoo-dyoñt*

stung piqué *peekay*

stupid stupide *stoopeed*

suddenly soudain *soodañ*

suede le daim *dañ*

sugar le sucre *sookr*

suit *(man's)* le costume *kostoom*; *(women's)* le tailleur *tye-yur*

suitcase la valise *valeez*

summer l'été *(m)* aytay*

sun le soleil *solay*

sunbathe prendre un bain de soleil *proñdr un bañ duh solay*

sunburn le coup de soleil *koo duh solay*

sunglasses les lunettes *(fpl)* de soleil *loonet duh solay*

sunny: it's sunny il fait du soleil *eel feh doo solay*

sunshade le parasol *para-sol*

sunstroke l'insolation *(f)* añso-la-syoñ*

suntan lotion le lait solaire *leh solehr*

supermarket le supermarché *soopehr-marshay*

supper *(dinner)* le souper *soopay*

supplement le supplément *sooplay-moñ*

sure sûr *soor*

surface mail par voie de terre *par vwa duh ter*

surfboard la planche de surf *ploñsh duh surf*

surfing le surf *surf*

surname le nom de famille *noñ duh fameey*

suspension la suspension *soospoñ-syoñ*

sweater le pull *pool*

sweet sucré *sookray*

sweetener l'édulcorant *(m)* aydoolko-roñ*

sweets les bonbons *(mpl)* boñboñ*

swim nager *nazhay*

swimming pool la piscine *peeseen*

swimsuit le maillot de bain *mye-yoh duh bañ*

Swiss suisse *swees*

switch le bouton *bootoñ*

switch off éteindre *ay-tañdr*

switch on allumer *aloomay*

Switzerland la Suisse *swees*

synagogue la synagogue *seena-gog*

table la table *tabl*

tablecloth la nappe *nap*

tablespoon la cuiller de service *kwee-yehr duh sehrvees*

tablet le comprimé *koñpree-may*

table tennis le ping-pong *ping-pong*

take prendre *proñdr*; **how long does it take?** ça prend combien de temps? *sa proñ koñbyoñ duh toñ*

talc le talc *talk*

talk parler *parlay*

tall grand *groñ*

tampons les tampons *(mpl)* toñpoñ*

tap le robinet *robee-nay*

tape le ruban *roobon̄*

tape-recorder le magnétophone *man-yeto-fon*

tartar sauce la sauce tartare *sohs tartar*

taste[1] *vb* : **can I taste some?** puis-je goûter? *pweezh gootay*

taste[2] *n* le goût *goo*

tax l'impôt *(m) an̄po*

taxi le taxi *taksee*

taxi rank la station de taxis *sta-syon̄ duh taksee*

tea le thé *tay*

tea bag le sachet de thé *sashay duh tay*

teach enseigner *on̄sehn-yay*

teacher le professeur *profeh-sur*

teapot la théière *tay-yehr*

teaspoon la cuiller à café *kwee-yehr a kafay*

teat la tétine *tayteen*

teeth les dents *(mpl)*

telegram le télégramme *taylaygram*

telephone le téléphone *taylay-fon*

telephone box la cabine téléphonique *kabeen taylay-foneek*

telephone call le coup de téléphone *koo duh taylay-fon*

telephone directory l'annuaire *(m) anwehr*

television la télévision *taylay-veezyon̄*

telex le télex *tayleks*

tell dire *deer*

temperature la température *ton̄pay-ratoor;* **to have a temperature** avoir de la fièvre *avwar duh la fyeh-vr*

temporary provisoire *proveez-wahr*

tennis le tennis *tenees*

tennis court le court de tennis *koor duh tenees*

tennis racket la raquette de tennis *ra-ket duh tenees*

tent la tente *ton̄t*

tent peg le piquet de tente *peekay duh ton̄t*

terminus le terminus *tehrmee-noos*

terrace la terrasse *teh-ras*

than que *kuh*

thank you merci *mehrsee;* **thank you very much** merci beaucoup *mehrsee bokoo*

that cela *suhla;* **that one** celui-là *suh-lwee-la*

thaw: it's thawing il dégèle *eel dayzhel*

theatre le théâtre *tayatr*

then alors *alor*

there là *la;* **there is/there are** il y a *eel ya*

thermometer le thermomètre *tehrmo-mehtr*

these ceux-ci *suh-see*

they ils/elles *eel/el; see* **GRAMMAR**

thief le voleur *vo-lur*

thing la chose *shohz;* **my things** mes affaires *mayz afehr*

think penser *pon̄say*

third troisième *trwa-zyem*

thirsty: I'm thirsty j'ai soif *zhay swaf*

this ceci *suhsee;* **this one** celui-ci *suh-lwee-see*

those ceux-là *suh-la*

thread le fil *feel*

throat la gorge *gorzh*

throat lozenges les pastilles *(fpl)* pour la gorge *pasteey poor la gorzh*

through à travers *a travehr*

thunderstorm l'orage *(m) orazh*

ticket le billet *bee-yay*

ticket collector le contrôleur *koñtroh-lur*

ticket office le guichet *gee-shay*

tide la marée *ma-ray*

tie la cravate *kra-vat*

tights le collant *koloñ*

till[1] *n* la caisse *kes*

till[2] *prep* jusqu'à *zhoo-ska*

time le temps *toñ*; **this time** cette fois *set fwah*

timetable board le tableau des horaires *tabloh dayz orehr*

tin la boîte *bwat*

tinfoil le papier d'étain *papyay daytañ*

tin-opener l'ouvre-boîtes *(m) oovr-bwat*

tip *(to waiter etc)* le pourboire *poorbwahr*

tipped filtre *filtr*

tired fatigué *fateegay*

tissue le kleenex ® *klee-neks*

to à *a*; *(with name of country)* en *on*

toast le toast *toast*

tobacco le tabac *taba*

tobacconist's le bureau de tabac *booro duh taba*

today aujourd'hui *oh-zhoor-dwee*

together ensemble *oñ-soñbl*

toilet les toilettes *(fpl) twalet*

toilet paper le papier hygiénique *papyay ee-zhay-neek*

toll le péage *pay-yazh*

tomato la tomate *tomat*

tomato juice le jus de tomate *zhoo duh tomat*

tomorrow demain *duhmañ*

tongue la langue *loñg*

tonic water le Schweppes ®

tonight ce soir *suh swahr*

too *(also)* aussi *oh-see*; **it's too big** c'est trop grand *seh troh groñ*

tooth la dent *doñ*

toothbrush la brosse à dents *bros a doñ*

toothpaste le dentifrice *doñtee-frees*

top[1] *adj* : **the top floor** le dernier étage *dehr-nyehr ay-tazh*

top[2] *n* le dessus *duhsoo*; **on top of** sur *soor*

torch la lampe de poche *loñp duh posh*

torn déchiré *dayshee-ray*

total le total *to-tal*

tough *(meat)* dur *door*

tour l'excursion *(f) ekskoor-syoñ*

tourist le/la touriste *tooreest*

tourist office le syndicat d'initiatif *sañdee-ka deenee-sya-teev*

tourist ticket le billet touristique *bee-yay toores-teek*

tow remorquer *ruhmor-kay*

towel la serviette *sehr-vyet*

town la ville *veel*

town centre le centre ville *soñtr veel*

town plan le plan de la ville *ploñ duh la veel*

tow rope le câble de remorque *kahbl duh ruhmork*

toy le jouet *zhoo-ay*

traditional traditionnel *tradee-syo-nel*

traffic la circulation *seerkoo-lasyoñ*
trailer la remorque *ruhmork*
train le train *trañ*
training shoes les chaussures *(fpl)* de sport *shohsoor duh spor*
tram le tramway *tramway*
translate traduire *tradweer*
translation la traduction *tradook-syoñ*
travel voyager *vwaya-zhay*
travel agent l'agent *(m)* de voyages *a-zhoñ duh vwa-yazh*
traveller's cheque le chèque de voyage *shek duh vwa-yazh*
tray le plateau *plato*
tree l'arbre *(m)* *arbr*
trip l'excursion *(f)* *ekskoor-syoñ*
trouble les ennuis *(mpl)* *oñ-nwee*
trousers le pantalon *poñta-loñ*
true vrai *vray*
trunk *(luggage)* la malle *mal*
trunks le slip (de bain) *sleep (duh bañ)*
try essayer *essay-yay*
try on essayer *essay-yay*
T-shirt le T-shirt *tee-shurt*
tuna le thon *toñ*
tunnel le tunnel *too-nel*
turkey le dindon *dañdoñ*
turn *(handle, wheel)* tourner *toornay*
turnip le navet *navay*
turn off *(light, etc)* éteindre *ay-tañdr*; *(engine)* arrêter le moteur *areh-tay luh mo-tur*
turn on *(light etc)* allumer *aloomay*; *(engine)* mettre en marche *metroñ marsh*

tweezers la pince à épiler *pañs a aypee-lay*
twice deux fois *duh fwah*
twin-bedded room la chambre à deux lits *shoñbra duh lee*
typical typique *teepeek*
tyre le pneu *p-nuh*
tyre pressure la pression des pneus *preh-syoñ day p-nuh*

umbrella le parapluie *para-plwee*
uncomfortable inconfortable *añkoñfor-tabl*
unconscious sans connaissance *soñ koneh-soñs*
under sous *soo*
underground le métro *maytroh*
underpass le passage souterrain *pasazh sootrañ*
understand comprendre *koñproñdr*; **I don't understand** je ne comprends pas *zhuh nuh koñproñ pa*
underwear les sous-vêtements *(mpl)* *soo-vetmoñ*
United States les États Unis *(mpl)* *aytaz oonee*
university l'université *(f)* *oonee-vehrsee-tay*
unpack *(case)* défaire *dayfehr*
up levé *luhvay*; **up there** là-haut *la-oh*
upstairs en haut *oñ oh*
urgent urgent *oor-zhoñ*
use utiliser *ooteelee-zay*
useful utile *ooteel*
usual habituel *abeetoo-el*
usually habituellement *abeetoo-el-moñ*

vacancy *(in hotel)* la chambre à louer *shoñbra looay*

vacuum cleaner l'aspirateur *(m) aspee-ra-tur*

valid valable *va-labl*

valley la vallée *valay*

valuable d'une grande valeur *doon groñd va-lur*

valuables les objets *(mpl)* de valeur *obzhay duh va-lur*

van la camionnette *kamyo-net*

vase le vase *vaz*

VAT la TVA *tay-vay-a*

veal le veau *voh*

vegetables les légumes *(mpl) laygoom*

vegetarian végétarien *vay-zhayta-ryañ*

ventilator le ventilateur *voñtee-la-tur*

vermouth le vermouth *vehrmoot*

very très *treh*

vest le maillot de corps *mye-yoh duh kor*

via par *par*

video *(recorder)* le magnétoscope *man-yayto-skop*

view la vue *voo*

villa la maison de campagne *mehzoñ duh koñ-panyuh*

village le village *veelazh*

vinegar le vinaigre *veenaygr*

vineyard le vignoble *vee-nyobl*

visa le visa *veeza*

visit visiter *veezeetay*

vitamin la vitamine *veetameen*

vodka la vodka *vodka*

voltage le voltage *voltazh*

waist la taille *tye*

wait (for) attendre *atoñdr*

waiter le garçon *garsoñ*

waiting room la salle d'attente *sal datoñt*

waitress la serveuse *sehr-vuz*

wake up se réveiller *suh rayvay-yay*

Wales le pays de Galles *payee duh gal*

walk[1] *vb* aller à pied *alay a pyay*

walk[2] *n* : **to go for a walk** faire une promenade *fehr oon promnad*

wallet le portefeuille *port-fuhy*

walnut la noix *nwa*

want désirer *dayzeeray*

warm chaud *shoh*

warning triangle le triangle de présignalisation *tree-yoñgl duh praysee-nyalee-za-syoñ*

wash laver *lavay*; **to wash oneself** se laver *suh lavay*

washbasin le lavabo *lava-boh*

washing machine la machine à laver *masheen a lavay*

washing powder la lessive *les-seev*

washing-up liquid le lave-vaisselle *lav-veh-sel*

wasp la guêpe *gep*

waste bin la poubelle *poobel*

watch[1] *n* la montre *moñtr*

watch[2] *vb* *(look at)* regarder *ruhgarday*

water l'eau *(f) oh*

waterfall la chute d'eau *shoot doh*

water heater le chauffe-eau *shohf-oh*

watermelon la pastèque *pastek*

waterproof imperméable *añ-pehr-may-yabl*

water-skiing le ski nautique *skee noteek*

wave *(on sea)* la vague *vag*

wax la cire *seer*

way *(manner)* la manière *man-yehr*; *(route)* le chemin *shuhmañ*; **this way** par ici *par eesee*

we nous *noo*; see **GRAMMAR**

weak faible *febl*

wear porter *portay*

weather le temps *toñ*

wedding le mariage *mar-yazh*

week la semaine *smen*

weekday le jour de semaine *zhoor duh smen*

weekend le weekend

weekly par semaine *par smen*

weight le poids *pwa*

welcome bienvenu *byañ-vuhnoo*

well en bonne santé *oñ bon soñtay*; **well done** *(steak)* bien cuit *byañ kwee*

Welsh gallois *galwa*

west l'ouest *(m)* west

wet mouillé *moo-yay*

wetsuit la combinaison de plongée *koñbee-nezoñ duh ploñ-zhay*

what quoi *kwa*; **what is it?** qu'est-ce que c'est? *kes kuh seh*

wheel la roue *roo*

wheelchair le fauteuil roulant *fohteu rooloñ*

when quand *koñ*

where où *oo*

which quel/quelle *kel*; **which is it?** c'est lequel/laquelle? *seh luhkel/lakel*

while pendant que *poñdoñ kuh*

whipped fouetté *fwetay*

whisky le whisky *weeskee*

white blanc/blanche *bloñ/bloñsh*

who qui *kee*

whole entier *oñ-tyay*

wholemeal: wholemeal bread le pain complet *pañ koñpleh*

whose: whose is it? c'est à qui? *sayt a kee*

why pourquoi *poorkwa*

wide large *larzh*

wife la femme *fam*

window la fenêtre *fuhnetr*; *(shop)* la vitrine *veetreen*

windscreen le pare-brise *parbreez*

windsurfing la planche à voile *ploñsh a vwal*

wine le vin *vañ*

wine list la carte des vins *kart day vañ*

winter l'hiver *(m)* eevehr

with avec *avek*

without sans *soñ*

woman la femme *fam*

wood le bois *bwa*

wool la laine *len*

word le mot *moh*

work *(person)* travailler *tra-vye-yay*; *(machine, car)* fonctionner *foñk-syonay*

worried inquiet *añ-kyay*

worse pire *peer*

worth: it's worth ... ça vaut ... *sa voh ...*

wrap (up) envelopper *oñ-vlopay*

wrapping paper le papier d'emballage *papyay doñba-lazh*

write écrire *aykreer*

writing paper le papier à lettres *papyay a letr*

wrong faux *foh*

yacht le yacht *yot*

year l'an *(m) oñ*

yellow jaune *zhohn*

yes oui *wee*; **yes please** oui merci *wee mehrsee*

yesterday hier *yehr*

yet: not yet pas encore *paz oñkor*

yoghurt le yaourt *ya-oort*

you vous *voo*; *(with friends)* tu *too*; *see* **GRAMMAR**

young jeune *zhuhn*

youth hostel l'auberge *(f)* de jeunesse *ohberzh duh zhuh-nes*

zero le zéro *zayro*

zip la fermeture éclair *fehrm-toor ayklehr*

zoo le zoo *zoh*

à to; at

abats *mpl* offal; giblets

abbaye *f* abbey

abonné(e) *m/f* subscriber; season ticket holder

abonnement *m* subscription; season ticket

abri *m* shelter

abricot *m* apricot

absence *f*: **absence de signalisation horizontale** no road markings; **absence (partielle) de marquage** no road markings (on some sections)

abus *m*: **tout abus sera puni** penalty for improper use

accès *m*: **l'accès de cette voiture ...** entrance to this carriage ...; **accès interdit** no entry; **accès réservé** authorized entrance only; **accès aux quais** to the trains

accessoires *mpl* accessories

accompagnateur(trice) *m/f* guide; courier

accompagnement *m* *(on menu)* accompanying vegetables

accompagné: enfants non accompagnés unaccompanied children

accotement *m* verge; **accotement meuble/non stabilisé** soft verge

accueil *m* reception

accueillir to greet; to welcome

accusé de réception *m* receipt *(for parcel)*

A.C.F. *m* Automobile Club de France

achat *m* purchase

acheter to buy

acier *m* steel

acompte *m* down payment; deposit

action *f* action; special offer *(Switz. only)*

actionner: actionnez le signal d'alarme operate the alarm

activité *f* activity

addition *f* bill

adhérent(e) *m/f* member

adjoint(e) *m/f* deputy

adresser to address; **s'adresser à/adressez-vous à** go and see *(person)*; enquire at *(office)*

aéroclub *m* flying club

aérogare *f* terminal

aéroglisseur *m* hovercraft

aéroport *m* airport

affaires *fpl* business; belongings; **bonnes affaires** bargains; **déjeuner/dîner d'affaires** business lunch/dinner

affections *fpl*: **affections respiratoires** respiratory diseases

affiche *f* poster; notice

afficher: défense d'afficher post no bills

affranchissement *m* postage; **dispensé d'affranchissement** postage paid

afin de in order to

âgé(e) elderly; **âgé de** aged

agence *f* agency; branch; **agence immobilière** estate agency; **agence de voyages** travel agency

agenda *m* diary

agent *m* agent; **agent de police** policeman

agiter: agiter avant emploi shake before use

agneau *m* lamb

agrandissement *m* enlargement

agréable pleasant; nice

agréé(e) registered; authorized

aide *f* help; **à l'aide de** with the help of

aiglefin *m* haddock

aigre sour; **à l'aigre-doux** sweet and sour

ail *m* garlic

aile *f* wing

ailloli *see* **aïoli**

aimable: notre aimable clientèle our customers

aïoli *m* garlic mayonnaise; poached cod with garlic mayonnaise

air: en plein air (in the) open air; **de plein air** outdoor

aire *f*: **aire de jeux** play area; **aire de repos** lay-by; **aire de services** service area; **aire de stationnement** lay-by

airelles *fpl* bilberries; cranberries

alcool *m* alcohol; fruit brandy; **alcool blanc** colourless brandy; **alcool à brûler** methylated spirits

alcoolisé(e) alcoholic; **non alcoolisé(e)** soft

algues *fpl* seaweed

aliment *m* food

alimentation *f* food; grocery shop

allée *f* driveway; **allée réservée aux cavaliers** path for horse-riding only

Allemagne *f* Germany

allemand(e) German

aller to go

aller-retour *m* return ticket

aller (simple) *m* single ticket

allumé(e) on; lit

allumer to turn on; to light; **allumez vos phares** switch on headlights

allumette *f* match; **(pommes) allumettes** matchstick potatoes

aloyau *m* sirloin

alpinisme *m* mountaineering; climbing

Alsace *f* region producing dry German-type white wines

alsacien(ne) Alsatian; **à l'alsacienne** usually served with sauerkraut, ham and sausages

altiport *m* mountain air strip

amande *f* almond; **pâte d'amandes** almond paste; marzipan

amandine *f* almond cake

ambassade *f* embassy

amélioration *f* improvement

aménagements *mpl* work(s)

amende *f* fine

amer(ère) bitter

américano *m* aperitif similar to red vermouth

ameublement *m* furniture

ami(e) *m/f* friend

amicale *f* association

amovible removable

amuse-gueule *m* appetizer

an *m* year

ananas *m* pineapple

anchois *m* anchovy

ancien(ne) old; former; **à l'ancienne** in a wine and cream sauce with mushrooms and onions

andalouse: à l'andalouse with green peppers, aubergines and tomatoes

andouille *f* sausage made of chitterlings

andouillette *f* small sausage made of chitterlings

anglais(e) English

Angleterre *f* England

anguille *f* eel

animateur/animatrice *m/f* group leader

animation *f* entertainment; activity

animaux *mpl* : **animaux admis/non admis** animals/no animals allowed

anis *m* aniseed

anisette *f* aniseed liqueur

année *f* year; vintage

anniversaire *m* anniversary; birthday

annonce *f* advertisement

annuaire *m* directory

annulation *f* cancellation

annuler to cancel

antenne *f* aerial

antillais(e) West Indian

antiquaire *m/f* antique dealer

antiquités *fpl* antiques

A.O.C. see **appellation**

août *m* August

appareil *m* appliance; camera

appareil-photo *m* camera

appartement *m* apartment; flat

appartement-témoin *m* showflat

appel *m* call

appellation *f* : **appellation d'origine contrôlée (A.O.C.)** mark guaranteeing the quality and origin of a wine

appétit *m* : **bon appétit!** enjoy your meal!

appoint *m* : **faire l'appoint** exact money please

appuyer: **appuyer sur** to push; **appuyez** push; **appuyez sur le bouton** press the button

après after

après-midi *m* afternoon

après-rasage *m* after-shave

arachide *f* groundnut

arbre *m* tree

argent *m* money; silver *(metal)*

argenterie *f* silverware

armagnac *m* dry brown brandy

aromates *mpl* seasoning; herbs

arrêt *m* stop; off *(machine)*; **arrêt d'autobus** bus stop; **arrêt facultatif** request stop

arrêté *m* : **par arrêté préfectoral/ municipal** by order of the prefect/ Town Council

arrêtez stop

arrhes *fpl* deposit *(part payment)*

arrière *m* rear; back

arrivage *m* : **arrivage d'huîtres** fresh oysters

arrivée *f* arrival

arrondissement *m* district *(in Paris)*

artichaut *m* artichoke; **coeur/fond d'artichaut** artichoke heart

article *m* item; article; **articles de toilette** toiletries

artisan *m* craftsman

artisanal(e) handmade

artisanat *m* arts and crafts

ascenseur *m* lift

asperge *f* asparagus

assaisonnement *m* seasoning; dressing

assiette f plate; **assiette anglaise** assorted cold roast meats; **assiette charcutière/de charcuterie** assorted cold meats; **assiette de crudités (de saison)** (seasonal) salads and raw vegetables; **assiette valaissane** 'viande séchée' served with rye bread, cheese and pickles

assise: place assise seat

assorti(e) assorted; matching

assortiment m assortment

assurance f insurance; **assurance tous-risques** comprehensive insurance; **assurance voyages** travel insurance

assuré(e) insured; **parking assuré** parking facilities; **desserte assurée par autocar** there is a bus service; **le service est assuré par la SNCF** there is a train service

assurer to assure; to insure; **ce train assure la correspondance avec le train de 16.45** this train connects with the 16.45; **s'assurer que** ensure that

atelier m workshop; artist's studio

attacher: attachez votre ceinture fasten seat belts

attendre to wait (for); wait!

attention look out!; **attention à la marche** mind the step; **attention au feu** danger of fire; **attention! vous n'avez pas la priorité** warning! give way to traffic from the right

attestation f: **attestation d'assurance** insurance certificate

attirer: nous attirons l'attention de notre aimable clientèle sur ... we would ask our customers/guests to note (that) ...

auberge f inn; **auberge de jeunesse** youth hostel

aubergine f aubergine; **aubergines farcies** stuffed aubergines; **aubergines à la grecque** aubergines cooked in olive oil with onion, coriander, rice and vinegar

aucun(e) none; no; not any

au-delà de beyond

au gratin with cheese topping

aujourd'hui today; **aujourd'hui le chef vous propose ...** the chef's special today is ...

au revoir goodbye

aussi also

autobus m bus

autocar m coach

auto-école f driving school

automne m autumn

automobiliste m/f motorist

autorisé(e) permitted; authorized

autoroute f motorway; **autoroute à péage** toll motorway

auto-stop m hitchhiking

autre other; **autres directions** other routes

avaler: ne pas avaler not to be taken internally

avance f: **à l'avance** in advance; **d'avance** in advance

avant before; front; **à l'avant** at the front

avec with

avertir to inform; to warn

aveugle blind

avion m plane

aviron m rowing (sport)

avis m : **sans avis médical** without

medical advice; **avis au public** notice to the public

avocat m avocado (pear); lawyer

avoine f oats

avoir to have

avril m April

baba au rhum m rum baba

bagages mpl luggage; **bagages accompagnés** registered luggage; **bagages à main** hand-luggage

baguette f stick of (French) bread

baignade f: **baignade interdite** no bathing; **baignade surveillée** supervised bathing

baigner: se baigner to bathe; to go swimming

baignoire f bath

bail m lease

bain m bath

bal m ball; dance

balade f walk; drive

balcon m circle (in theatre); balcony

balisé(e) signposted

ballon m balloon; ball; glass of wine (1 decilitre)

ballottine f: **ballottine de volaille/d'agneau** meat loaf made with poultry/lamb

ball-trap m clay pigeon shooting

banane f banana; **bananes flambées** bananas served in flaming brandy

bande f line; **bande d'arrêt d'urgence** hard shoulder

banlieue f suburbs; **de banlieue** suburban

banque f bank

bar¹ m bar; **bar à café** unlicensed bar (Switz.)

bar² m bass (fish)

barbue f brill

barquette f punnet; small tart

barrage m dam; **barrage routier** road block

barré: route barrée road closed

barrer to cross out

barrière automatique f automatic turnstile; automatic barrier

Barsac m sweet white wine from Bordeaux

bas m bottom (of page, list, etc); stocking; **en bas** below; downstairs

bas(se) low

basilic m basil

basquaise: poulet à la basquaise chicken in sauce of tomato, onion, pepper, garlic and parsley, served with rice

bassin m pond

bâtard m type of Vienna loaf

batavia f Webb lettuce

bateau m boat; ship; **bateau de plaisance** pleasure boat; **bateau-mouche** river boat; pleasure steamer

bâtiment m building

bâtonnet glacé m ice lolly

bavaroise f type of mousse

bavette (échalotes) f type of steak with shallots

bazar m general store

Beaujolais m light, fruity wine to be drunk young

béarnaise in a thick sauce made with butter, egg yolks, shallots, vinegar and herbs

beau lovely; fine

beaucoup much; **beaucoup de**

many; much/a lot of

bébé *m* baby

bécasse *f* woodcock

bécassine *f* snipe

béchamel *f* white sauce

beignet *m* fritter; doughnut

Belgique *f* Belgium

belle lovely

belon *m* Belon oyster

belvédère *m* panoramic viewpoint

Bénédictine *f* greenish-yellow liqueur

benne *f* cable-car

Bercy *f* sauce made with white wine, shallots and butter

Bergerac *m* red and white wines from the Dordogne

berlingots *mpl* boiled sweets

besoin *m* : **en cas de besoin** if necessary

betterave *f* beetroot

beurre *m* butter; **beurre d'anchois** anchovy paste; **beurre blanc** butter sauce made with white wine, shallots and vinegar; **beurre laitier** dairy butter; **beurre maître d'hôtel** melted butter with parsley and lemon juice; **beurre noir** brown butter sauce

bibliothèque *f* library

bicyclette *f* bicycle

bien well; right; good

bientôt soon; shortly

bière *f* beer; **bière blonde** lager; **bière brune** bitter; **bière à la pression** draught beer

bifteck *m* steak; **bifteck tartare** minced raw steak with raw egg, onion, tartar or Worcester sauce and capers

bigarade *f* orange sauce with sugar and vinegar

bigarreau *m* bigarreau cherry

bigorneau *m* winkle

bijoux *mpl* jewellery; **bijoux (de) fantaisie** costume jewellery

bijouterie *f* jeweller's (shop); jewellery

billet *m* ticket; note; **billet aller-retour** return ticket; **billet de banque** bank note; **billet simple** one-way ticket

biscotte *f* breakfast biscuit; rusk

biscuit *m* biscuit; **biscuit à la cuiller** sponge finger; **biscuit de Savoie** sponge cake

bisque *f*: **bisque de homard/ d'écrevisses** lobster/crayfish soup

blanc white; blank; **blanc (de poulet)** breast of chicken; **laissez en blanc** leave blank

Blanc de Blancs *m* any white wine made from white grapes only

blanche white; blank

blanchisserie *f* laundry

blanquette *f*: **blanquette de veau/ d'agneau** stewed veal/lamb in white sauce

Blanquette de Limoux *m* dry, sparkling white wine from the south-west

blé *m* wheat; **blé noir** buckwheat

bleu(e) blue; very rare *(steak)*; **bleu d'Auvergne** rich blue cheese, sharp and salty; **bleu de Bresse** mild, soft blue cheese; **bleu marine** navy blue

blonde light (beer)

bloquer to block; **bloquer le passage** to be in the way

bock m glass of beer

boeuf m beef; **boeuf bourguignon** beef stew in red wine; **boeuf en daube** beef casserole; **boeuf miroton** boiled beef in onion sauce; **boeuf à la mode** beef braised in red wine with vegetables and herbs

boire to drink

bois m wood

boisson f drink; **boissons chaudes/ fraîches** hot/cold drinks

boîte f can; box; **en boîte** canned; **boîte d'allumettes** box of matches; matchbox; **boîte aux lettres** letter box; **boîte de nuit** night club

bolée f bowl; cup

bolet m boletus mushroom

bombe f aerosol; **bombe glacée** ice pudding

bon m token; voucher; **bon de commande** order form

bon(ne) good; right; **bon marché** cheap

bonbon m sweet; **bonbon à la menthe** mint

bonjour hello; good morning/ afternoon

bonne see **bon(ne)**

bonneterie f hosiery

bonsoir good evening

bord m border; edge; verge; **à bord** on board; **le bord de (la) mer** seaside

Bordeaux m claret

bordeaux maroon

bordelaise: à la bordelaise in a red wine sauce with shallots, beef marrow and mushrooms

bordier m : **bordiers autorisés** local traffic only (Switz.)

bordure f border

botte f boot; bunch

bottin m directory

bouche d'incendie f fire hydrant

bouchée f chocolate; **bouchée à la reine** chicken vol-au-vent

boucherie f butcher's shop; **boucherie chevaline** horsemeat butcher's

boucle d'oreille f earring

boudin m black pudding; **boudin blanc** white pudding; **boudin aux pommes** black pudding with apple

boudoir m sponge finger

boue f mud

bouée de sauvetage f lifebelt

bouillabaisse f rich fish soup or stew

bouillir to boil

bouillon m stock

boulangerie f bakery

boule f ball; **boules** game similar to bowls played on rough ground with metal bowls; **boule (de glace)** scoop of ice cream; **boule de gomme** throat pastille; fruit pastille

boulette f dumpling

Bourgogne f Burgundy

Bourgueuil m light, fruity red wine to be drunk young

bourguignon(ne) in a sauce made with red wine, onions, herbs and spices

Bourse f stock exchange

bout m end

bouteille f bottle

boutique f shop

bouton m button; switch

box m lock-up garage

boxe f boxing

braderie f clearance sale

braisé(e) braised

brandade (de morue) f poached cod with garlic and parsley

brasserie f brewery; café

Bretagne f Brittany

breton(ne) from Brittany

bricolage m do-it-yourself

brie m soft, mild cow's-milk cheese

brioche f brioche (soft roll made with a very light dough); **brioche sucrée** sugared brioche

briocherie f bakery/café specialising in brioches, croissants etc

briser: brisez la glace/vitre break the glass

britannique British

brocante f second-hand goods; flea market

broche f brooch; spit; **à la broche** spit-roasted

brochet m pike

brochette f skewer; kebab

brodé main hand-embroidered

bronzage m suntan

brouillard m fog

brugnon m nectarine

bruit m noise

brûlot m sugar flamed in brandy and added to coffee

brun(e) brown; dark

brushing m blow-dry

brut(e) gross; raw; **(champagne) brut** dry champagne

Bruxelles Brussels

bulletin de consigne m left-luggage ticket

bureau m desk; office; **bureau de change** (foreign) exchange office; **bureau de poste** post office; **bureau de tabac** tobacconist's shop

butagaz ® m Calor gas ®

buvette f refreshment room; refreshment stall

cabillaud m (fresh) cod; **cabillaud au gratin** cod, béchamel sauce and cheese topping

cabine f cabin; cubicle; **cabine d'essayage** changing room; **cabine téléphonique** telephone booth; **cette cabine peut être appelée à ce numéro** for incoming calls give this number

cabinet m office; **cabinet médical/ dentaire** doctor's/dentist's surgery; **cabinet de toilette** toilet

cacahuète f peanut

cacao m cocoa

cadeau m gift

cadre m picture frame; surroundings

café m coffee; café; **café crème** white coffee; **café décaféiné** decaffeinated coffee; **café au lait** white coffee; **café lyophilisé** freeze-dried coffee; **café noir** black coffee; **café en poudre** instant coffee

cafetière f coffee pot

caille f quail

caisse f checkout; cash desk; case; **caisse d'épargne** savings bank

caissier(ière) m/f cashier; teller

cake m fruit cake

calendrier m calendar; timetable

calisson (d'Aix) m small lozenge-shaped sweetmeat made of almond paste with icing on top

calmar m squid

calvados m apple brandy

camembert m soft creamy cheese from Normandy

campagne f country; countryside; campaign

camping m camping; camp-site; **camping sauvage** camping on unofficial sites

camping-car m camper (van)

camping-gaz m camping stove

canapé m sofa; open sandwich

canard m duck; **canard à l'orange/ aux olives** duck in orange sauce/ with olives

caneton m : **caneton rôti** roast duckling

cannelle f cinnamon

canot m boat; **canot de sauvetage** lifeboat

canotage m boating

cantal m hard strong cheese from Cantal in the Auvergne

canton m state (Switz.)

câpres fpl capers

car m coach

caractère m character

carafe f carafe; decanter

caramel m toffee; caramel

carnaval m carnival

carnet m notebook; book

carnotzet m room in restaurant esp. for groups, serving mainly cheese dishes (Switz.)

carotte f carrot; **carottes râpées** grated carrot in vinaigrette; **carottes Vichy** carrots cooked in water and served with butter

carpe f carp

carré m square; **carré d'agneau/de porc** loin of lamb/pork; **carré de l'Est** cow's-milk cheese similar to camembert but milder

carrefour m intersection; crossroads

carrelet m plaice

carrière f quarry

carte f map; card; menu; **carte d'abonnement** season ticket; **carte bleue** credit card; **carte grise** logbook; **carte du jour** menu of the day; **carte nominative** card with named user; **carte orange** monthly or yearly season ticket; **carte postale** postcard; **carte routière** road map; **carte vermeille** senior citizen's rail pass; **carte des vins** wine list; **carte de voeux** greetings card

cartouche f carton (of cigarettes)

cas m case; **en cas de** in case of

cascade f waterfall

case postale f P.O. Box (Switz.)

caserne f barracks; **caserne de pompiers** fire station

casier m rack; locker

casque m helmet; **casque (à écouteurs)** headphones

casse-croûte *m* snack

cassis *m* blackcurrant; blackcurrant liqueur

cassolette *f* individual fondue dish

cassonade *f* brown sugar

cassoulet (toulousain) *m* stew made with beans, pork or mutton and sausages

catch *m* wrestling

cause *f* cause; **pour cause de** on account of

caution *f* security *(for loan)*; deposit; **caution à verser** deposit required

cave *f* cellar

caveau *m* cellar

caviar *m* caviar(e); **caviar d'aubergines** spread made with aubergines, garlic, olive oil and onions

C.D. = **chemin départemental**

céder to give in; **cédez la priorité/le passage** give way *(to traffic)*

cédratine *f* citron-based liqueur

C.E.E. *f* E.E.C.

ceinture *f* belt

céleri *m* celeriac; celery; **céleri rémoulade** celeriac in dressing

céleri-rave *m* celeriac

célibataire single

cendre *f* ash; **sous la cendre** cooked in the embers

cendrier *m* ashtray

cent hundred

centre *m* centre; **centre commercial** shopping centre; **centre équestre** riding school; **centre hospitalier** hospital complex; **centre de sports et loisirs** leisure centre; **centre ville** city centre

cèpes *mpl* boletus mushrooms

cercle *m* circle; ring

cerfeuil *m* chervil

cerise *f* cherry

cervelle *f* brains *(as food)*

cesser to stop

c'est it/he/she is

cette this; that

ceux the ones

ceux-ci these

ceux-là those

C.F.F. *mpl* Swiss Railways

Chablis *m* dry, full-bodied white wine

chaîne *f* chain; channel; (mountain) range; **chaîne hi-fi/ haute fidélité** hi-fi; **chaînes obligatoires** snow chains compulsory

chaise *f* chair; **chaise haute/de bébé** highchair; **chaise longue** deckchair

chalet *m* : **chalet-refuge** hut for skiers or hill-walkers; **chalet-skieurs** hut for skiers

Chambertin *m* full-bodied red wine

chambre *f* bedroom; room; **chambre à coucher** bedroom; **chambre d'enfants** nursery; **chambre individuelle** single room

champ *m* field; **champ de courses** racecourse

champenoise: méthode champenoise champagne-style

champignon *m* mushroom; **champignon de Paris** button mushroom; **champignons à la grecque** mushrooms in oil, wine and herbs

championnat *m* championship

change *m* exchange

changement *m* change; **changement de garniture: 5F** charge for change of vegetables: 5F

changer to alter; **changer de** to change

chanson *f* song

chanterelle *f* chanterelle *(mushroom)*

chantier *m* building site; roadworks

Chantilly: crème Chantilly whipped cream

chapelle *f* chapel

chapelure *f* (dried) breadcrumbs

chaque each; every

charcuterie *f* pork butcher's shop and delicatessen; cooked pork meats

charge *f* : **à votre charge** payable by you; **charges comprises** inclusive of service charges

chariot *m* trolley

charter *m* charter flight

chartreuse *f* yellow liqueur made from herbs and flowers

chasse *f* hunting; shooting; **chasse gardée** private hunting; private shooting

chasse-neige *m* snowplough

chasseur in a sauce made with white wine, shallots, tomatoes and mushrooms

châtaigne *f* chestnut

château *m* castle; mansion

chateaubriand *m* thick fillet steak, barded and lightly cooked in

butter

Châteauneuf du Pape *m* full-bodied red wine from the Rhône

chaud(e) warm; hot

chaud-froid *m* jellied sauce used to coat cooked meats, chicken etc

chauffage *m* heating

chauffeur *m* chauffeur; driver

chaussée *f* carriageway; **chaussée déformée** uneven road surface; **chaussée rétrécie** road narrows; **chaussée verglacée** icy/slippery road

chausson *m* : **chausson aux pommes** apple turnover

chaussure *f* shoe; boot

chef *m* chef; chief; head; leader

chef-lieu *m* : **chef-lieu de département** county town

chemin *m* path; lane; track; **chemin départemental** B-road; **chemin de fer** railway

chemise *f* shirt

chemisier *m* blouse

chèque *m* cheque; **chèque postal** post office Girocheque; **chèque de voyage** traveller's cheque

chèque-cadeau *m* gift token

cher (chère) dear; expensive

cherry *m* cherry brandy

cheval *m* horse

cheveux *mpl* hair

chèvre *f* goat; **fromage de chèvre** goat's milk cheese

chevreau *m* kid *(leather)*

chevreuil *m* roe deer; venison

chez at the house of

chicorée *f* chicory *(for coffee)*; endive; **chicorée braisée** braised endive

chien m dog; **chien méchant** beware of the dog

chips fpl crisps

chirurgien m surgeon

chocolat m chocolate; drinking chocolate; **chocolat à croquer** plain chocolate; **chocolat au lait** milk chocolate

choix m range; choice; **dessert au choix** choice of desserts

chope f tankard

chou m cabbage; **chou à la crème** cream puff; **choux de Bruxelles** Brussels sprouts

choucroute f sauerkraut; **choucroute garnie** sauerkraut served with boiled potatoes and assorted pork meats

chou-fleur m cauliflower

chou-rave m kohlrabi

C.H.U. m hospital

chute f fall; **risque de chute de pierres** danger: falling rocks; **chutes (d'eau)** waterfall

ciboulette f chives

cidre m cider

ciel m sky

cimetière m cemetery; graveyard

cinq five

cinquante fifty

cintre m coat hanger

cirage m shoe polish

circuit m (round) trip; circuit; **circuit touristique** excursion; scenic route

circulation f traffic; **circulation automobile interdite** no vehicular traffic

cirque m circus

cité f city; housing estate

citron m lemon; **citron pressé** fresh lemon drink; **citron vert** lime

citronnade f still lemonade

civet m : **civet de lapin/de lièvre/ d'oie** rich rabbit/hare/goose stew with red wine and onions

clafoutis m fruit, especially cherries, cooked in batter

clair(e) clear; light

claire f fattened oyster

classe f grade; class; **classe affaires** business class

clé f key; **clé de contact** ignition key; **clé minute** keys cut while you wait

clef see **clé**

client(e) m/f guest (at hotel); client; customer

clientèle f customers; clientele

climat m climate

climatisé(e) air-conditioned

clinique f nursing home, (private) clinic

clou m : **clou de girofle** clove

cocher to tick

cochon m pig; **cochon de lait** suckling pig

cocotte f casserole dish

cocotte-minute f pressure cooker

code m : **code de la route** Highway Code

coeur m heart; **coeurs de laitue/de palmiers** lettuce/palm hearts

coffre-fort m strongbox; safe

coiffeur m hairdresser; barber

coiffeuse f hairdresser; dressing table

coiffure f hair-style

coin m corner; **coin cuisine** kitchen area

cointreau m orange-based liqueur

col m collar; pass (in mountains); **col fermé en hiver** pass closed in winter

colin m hake

colis m parcel

collant m tights

collège m secondary school

coller to stick; to glue

collier m necklace; dog collar

colonie (de vacances) f holiday camp (for children)

combien how much/many

combustible m fuel

comique m comedian

commande f order; **sur commande** to order

commerçant(e) m/f trader

commerce m commerce; business; trade

commissariat de police m police station

communication f: **obtenir la communication** to get through; **communication interurbaine** trunk call; **communication urbaine** local call

compagnie f firm; **compagnie d'aviation** airline

compartiment m : **compartiment non-fumeur** non-smoking compartment

complet(ète) full (up)

composer to dial

composter: à composter to be date stamped/punched (ticket); **pour**

valider votre billet: compostez-le your ticket is not valid unless date-stamped/punched

compote f stewed fruit

comprenant including

comprimé m tablet

compris(e) including; **service compris** inclusive of service; **tout compris** all inclusive; **... non compris** exclusive of ...

comptant m : **payer (au) comptant** to pay cash

compte m account

compteur m speedometer; meter; **couper le courant/l'eau au compteur** to turn the electricity/water off at the mains

comptoir m bar; **au comptoir** at the bar; at the counter

comté m cheese similar to **gruyère**

concentré m : **concentré de tomate** tomato purée

concessionnaire m agent; distributor

concierge m/f caretaker; janitor

concombre m cucumber

concours m contest; aid

conducteur(trice) m/f driver

conduite f driving; behaviour

confection f ready-to-wear clothes

confiance f confidence; **de confiance** reliable

confirmer to confirm

confiserie f confectioner's shop

confit(e): fruits confits crystallized fruits

confit m : **confit d'oie/de canard** conserve of goose/of duck

confiture f jam; **confiture d'oranges**

marmalade; **confiture d'oignons** sweet and sour onion preserve

conformément à in accordance with

confort m comfort; **tout confort** all mod cons

congélateur m freezer

congelé(e) frozen

congre m conger eel

conseil m advice; **conseil municipal/régional** town/regional council; **conseils pratiques** practical advice; handy hints

conservation f: **longue conservation** long-life (milk etc)

conserve f canned food

conserver to keep; **conservez votre titre de transport jusqu'à la sortie** keep your ticket until you leave the station

consigne f deposit; left-luggage office; **consigne automatique** left-luggage lockers; **consignes de sécurité** safety instructions

consigné(e): bouteille consignée/ non consignée returnable/non-returnable bottle

consommateur(trice) m/f consumer

consommation f consumption; drink

consommé m clear soup

consommer: à consommer avant ... eat before ...

constat m report; **constat à l'amiable** jointly agreed statement for insurance purposes

contacter to contact

contenu m contents

contournement m bypass

contrat m contract; **contrat de location** lease

contravention f fine; parking ticket

contre against; versus

contre-filet m sirloin

contre-ordre m : **sauf contre-ordre** unless otherwise stated

contrôle m check; **contrôle radar** radar trap

contrôler: contrôlez ... check ...

contrôleur m ticket inspector

convenance f : **à votre convenance** when it suits you

conventionné(e): médecin conventionné = National Health Service; **prix conventionnés** prices in line with official guidelines

convenu(e) agreed

convoi m : **convoi exceptionnel** wide (or dangerous) load

coq m cock(erel); **coq au vin** chicken in red wine with mushrooms, bacon and garlic

coque f shell; cockle; **à la coque** soft boiled (egg)

coquelet m cockerel

coquet(te) pretty (place etc)

coquillages mpl shellfish

coquille f shell; **coquille Saint-Jacques** scallop; **coquilles de poisson** fish served in scallop shells

coquillettes fpl pasta shells

corail m coral; type of train without compartments

corbeille f basket

cordonnerie f shoe repairer's

shop; shoe repairing

cornet *m* cone

corniche *f* coast road

cornichon *m* gherkin

corps *m* body

correspondance *f* connection with other lines; correspondence

correspondant(e) *m/f* person phoning (or being phoned)

corrida *f* bullfight

Corse *f* Corsica

côte *f* coast; hill; rib; **côte de boeuf** rib of beef; **côte de porc (charcutière)** pork chop (with tomato and mushroom sauce); **côte de veau/d'agneau** veal/lamb cutlet

côté *m* side; **à côté de** beside; **à côté** nearby; next door

Côte d'Azur *f* Riviera

côtelette *f* cutlet; **côtelette de porc/d'agneau/de veau/de mouton** pork/lamb/veal/mutton chop

Côtes de Beaune *m* full-bodied red wine from Burgundy

Côtes du Rhône *m* full-bodied red wine from the Rhône

Côtes du Roussillon *m* good ordinary red wine

cotisation *f* subscription

cou *m* neck

couchage *m* : **sac de couchage** sleeping bag; **couchage 5 personnes** sleeps 5

couchette *f* couchette; bunk

couette *f* continental quilt

couler: faire couler to turn on (*water*)

couleur *f* colour

coulis *m* purée

couloir *m* corridor; **couloir d'autobus** bus lane

coulommiers *m* creamy white cow's-milk cheese, similar to **camembert**

coup *m* stroke; shot; blow; **coup de soleil** sunburn

coupe *f* goblet; dish; cup (*trophy*); **coupe (de cheveux)** haircut (*style*); **coupe de fruits** fruit salad; **coupe glacée** ice cream and fruit

coupure *f* cut; **coupure de courant** power cut

cour *f* court; courtyard

courant *m* power; current; **pour couper le courant** in order to cut off the power

courant(e) common; standard; current

courge *f* marrow (*vegetable*)

couronne *f* crown

courrier *m* mail; post

courroie *f* strap

cours *m* lesson; course; rate; **cours particuliers** private lessons; **en cours de validité** valid

course *f* race (*sport*); errand; **les courses** the races; **faire les courses** to go shopping; **course de taureaux** bullfight

court(e) short; **à court** short term

court-bouillon *m* stock for fish, made with root vegetables and white wine or vinegar

couscous *m* spicy Arab dish of steamed semolina with a meat stew

coût m cost

couteau m knife

coûteux(euse) expensive

couture f sewing

couvent m convent; monastery

couvert m cover charge; place setting; **couvert gratuit** no cover charge; **couvert, vin et service compris** cover charge, wine and service included

couvert(e) covered

couverture f blanket; cover; wrapper

cravate f (neck) tie

crayon m pencil

crèche f day nursery

crédit m credit; **à crédit** on credit; **la maison ne fait pas crédit** no credit given here

crème f cream; **un (café) crème** white coffee; **à la crème** with cream; **crème anglaise** custard; **crème de cacao** sweet liqueur with a chocolate flavour; **crème caramel** egg custard topped with caramel; **crème Chantilly** whipped cream; **crème fouettée** whipped cream; **crème glacée** ice cream; **crème pâtissière** confectioner's custard; **crème renversée** cream mould; **crème pour le visage** face cream

crémerie f dairy

crêpe f pancake; **crêpe flambée** pancake served in flaming brandy; **crêpe fourrée** stuffed pancake; **crêpe Suzette** pancake with orange sauce, served in flaming brandy (and often orange liqueur)

crêperie f pancake shop/restaurant

cresson m watercress

crevette f shrimp; **crevettes grises au beurre** potted shrimps; **crevette rose** prawn

croisière f cruise

croix f cross

croquant(e) crisp; crunchy

croque au sel f: **à la croque au sel** with a sprinkling of salt

croque-madame m toasted cheese sandwich with ham and fried egg

croque-monsieur m toasted ham and cheese sandwich

crottin de Chavignol m type of goat's-milk cheese

croustade f pastry shell with filling

croustillant(e) crisp

croûte f crust; **en croûte** in a pastry crust

C.R.S. mpl French riot police

crudités fpl selection of salads and raw vegetables

cru(e) raw; **premier cru** first-class wine; **cru classé** classified wine; **un vin de grand cru** a vintage wine

crustacés mpl shellfish

cuiller f spoon; **cuiller à café** teaspoon

cuillère see **cuiller**

cuir m leather

cuisine f cooking; cuisine; kitchen; **cuisine familiale** home cooking; **cuisine fine** high-class cuisine

cuisinier m cook

cuisinière f cook; cooker

cuisse f thigh; **cuisses de grenouille** frogs' legs; **cuisse de poulet** chicken leg

cuissot m haunch of venison/wild boar

cuit(e) done
cuivre m copper
culotte f panties
culturisme m body-building
cure f course of treatment; **cure thermale** course of treatment at a spa
cuvée f vintage
cyclomoteur m moped
cylindrée f (cubic) capacity (of engine)

d'abord at first
d'accord okay (agreement)
dacquoise f meringue dessert with fruit and cream
dactylo m/f typist
daim m suede
dames fpl ladies' (toilets)
dans into; in; on
dansant(e): soirée dansante dinner-dance
darne f thick fish steak
date f date (day)
datte f date (fruit)
daube f stew
daurade f sea bream; **daurade à la crème** sea bream in cream and mushroom sauce
de from; of
dé m dice; **en dés** diced
débarcadère m landing stage
débit m debit; **débit de boissons** drinking establishment
debout standing; upright
début m beginning
débutant(e) m/f beginner
décapsuleur m bottle opener

décembre m December
décès m death
décharge f: **décharge publique** rubbish dump
déchargement m unloading
déci m 1 decilitre of wine (Switz.)
déclaration f statement; report
déclarer: rien à déclarer nothing to declare
déclencher to set off (alarm)
décliner: décliner toute responsabilité to accept no responsibility
décollage m takeoff
décolleté m low neck
décongeler to defrost
décontracté(e) relaxed; casual
décortiqué(e) shelled
découverte f discovery
décrocher: décrochez lift the receiver
dédouaner to clear through customs
déduire to deduct
défaillance f (mechanical) failure
défaut m fault; defect
défectueux(euse) imperfect; faulty
défense f: **défense d'entrer** no entry; **défense de fumer** no smoking; **défense de marcher sur les pelouses** do not walk on the grass; **défense de stationner** no parking
dégager to clear
dégâts mpl damage
degré m degree
dégriffé(e): vêtements dégriffés designer seconds
dégustation f tasting

dehors outside; outdoors

déjeuner m lunch; breakfast *(Switz. only)*; **petit déjeuner** breakfast

délai m : **dans le délai fixé** within the time limit stipulated

délestage m : **itinéraire de délestage** alternative route avoiding heavy traffic

délit m offence; **tout délit sera passible d'amende** all offences will be punishable by a fine

délivré(e) issued *(passport etc)*

demain tomorrow

demande f application; **demandes d'emploi** situations wanted; **sur demande** on request

demander to ask (for)

démaquillant m make-up remover

démarqué(e) reduced *(goods)*

déménagement m : **entreprise de déménagement** removal firm

demi(e) half; **un demi** approx. half pint of draught beer *(France)*; half litre of wine *(Switz.)*

demi-pension f half board

demi-sec medium-dry

demi-sel slightly salted

demi-tarif m half-fare

déneigé(e) cleared of snow

dent f tooth

dentifrice m toothpaste

dépannage m : **service de dépannage** breakdown service

départ m departure; **au départ** at the start; at the place of departure; **au départ de** (leaving) from

département m department; regional division *(France)*

dépassement m : **dépassement**

interdit no overtaking; **dépassement dangereux** overtaking dangerous

dépasser to exceed; to overtake; **ne pas dépasser la dose prescrite** do not exceed the prescribed dose

dépenses fpl expenditure; outgoings

dépliant m brochure

déposé(e): marque déposée registered trademark; **modèle déposé** registered design

déposer: défense de déposer des ordures dumping of rubbish prohibited

dépositaire m/f agent

dépôt m deposit

dépôt m depot; **dépôt d'ordures** rubbish dump; **dépôt de pain** bread sold here

depuis since

dérangement m : **en dérangement** out of order

déranger to disturb

dernier(ère) last; **les dernières nouvelles** the latest news

derrière at the back; behind

dès from; since; **dès votre arrivée** as soon as you arrive

descendre to come/go down; to get/take down

désirer to want

désistement m withdrawal

désodorisant m air freshener

désolé(e) sorry

desserte f : **la desserte du village est assurée par autocar** there is a coach service to the village

dessin m : **dessin animé** cartoon *(animated)*

dessous underneath

dessus on top; **au dessus (de)** above

destinataire m/f addressee

destination f destination; **à destination de** bound for

détacher: détachez le coupon tear off the coupon; **détachez suivant le pointillé** tear off along the dotted line

détail m : **au détail** retail; **prix de détail** retail price

détaxé(e): produits détaxés duty free goods

détente f relaxation

détourner to divert

deux two; **les deux** both

deuxième second

deux-pièces m two-piece *(suit, swimsuit)*; two-roomed flat

deux-roues m two-wheeled vehicle

devant in front (of)

déviation f diversion

devis m quotation *(price)*

devises (étrangères) fpl foreign currency

dévisser to unscrew

diable in a hot, spicy sauce made with cayenne pepper, white wine, herbs and vinegar

diabolo m lemonade and fruit or mint cordial

diapositive f slide

diététique dietary; health foods

difficile difficult

digue f dyke; jetty

dimanche m Sunday

dinde f turkey; **dinde aux marrons** turkey with chestnut stuffing

dindonneau m young turkey

dîner m dinner; dinner party; lunch *(Switz.)*; **dîner aux chandelles** candlelit dinner; **dîner spectacle** cabaret dinner

diplomate m diplomat; type of trifle

diplômé(e) qualified

direct(e): train direct through train

directeur m manager; headmaster

direction f management; direction; **toutes directions** through traffic; all routes

directrice f manageress; headmistress

discrétion f : **discrétion assurée** discretion guaranteed; **vin à discrétion** unlimited wine

dispensé exempt from

disponible available

disposition f : **à votre disposition** at your service

disque m record; disc

distractions fpl entertainment

distributeur m : **distributeur automatique** vending machine; **prenez un ticket au distributeur** take a ticket from the machine

divers(e) various

dix ten

docteur m doctor

doigt m finger

domicile m home; address

donner to give; to give away

dorade *see* **daurade**

doré(e) golden

dossier m file

douane f customs

doubler to overtake

douce gentle; soft; mild

doucement quietly; gently

douche f shower

Douvres Dover

doux gentle; soft; mild

douzaine f dozen

dragée f sugared almond; sugar-coated pill

drap m sheet

droguerie f hardware shop

droit m right (entitlement); **droits de douane** customs duty

droit(e) right (not left); straight

droite f right-hand side; **à droite** on/to the right; **tourner à droite** to turn right

dur(e) hard; hard-boiled

durée f length (of time or stay)

duvet m sleeping bag

eau f water; **eau gazeuse/plate** fizzy/still water; **eau de Javel** bleach; **eau du robinet** tap-water; **eau-de-vie** brandy

échalote f shallot

échangeur m interchange

échantillon m sample

éclairage m lighting

écluse f lock (in canal)

école f school

économies fpl savings

écorce f peel (of orange, lemon)

Ecossais(e) m/f Scot; **écossais(e)** Scottish

écouteur m receiver

écran m screen; **bientôt sur les écrans** coming soon

écrevisse f crayfish (freshwater); **écrevisses à la nage** crayfish in white wine, vegetables and herbs

écrire to write; **écrire en caractères d'imprimerie** to write in block capitals

écrit: par écrit in writing

écurie f stable

éditeur(trice) m/f publisher

effet m : **prendre effet** to take effect

efficace effective; efficient

églefin m haddock

église f church

électro-ménager m household electrical appliances

élément m unit; element

elle she; her; it

elles they; them

éloigné(e) distant

emballage m packing

embarquement m boarding; **carte d'embarquement** boarding pass

embouteillage m traffic jam

émincé m thinly sliced meat/fruit in a sauce

émis(e) issued (ticket)

émission f programme; broadcast; issue (of ticket)

emmental m hard Swiss cheese, similar to **gruyère**

empêchement m : **en cas d'empêchement ...** in case of any problem ...

emplacement m : **emplacement réservé aux taxis etc** parking area reserved for taxis etc

emploi *m* use; job

emporter: à emporter take-away

emprunter: empruntez l'itinéraire ... follow the route ...

en some; any; in; to; **en panne** out of order; **en train/voiture** by train/car

en-cas *m* snack

enceinte pregnant

encore still; yet

encornet *m* squid

endives *fpl* chicory

endroit *m* place; spot

enfant *m* child

enlèvement *m* : **enlèvement et livraison de bagages à domicile** luggage collected from and delivered to your home

enneigement *m* snowfall; **bulletin d'enneigement** snow report

ennui *m* nuisance; trouble

enregistrement *m* : **enregistrement des bagages** check-in (desk)

enregistrer to record; to check in

enrobé(e): enrobé(e) de chocolat/caramel chocolate-/caramel-coated

enseignement *m* education

ensemble together

ensoleillé(e) sunny

entier(ère) whole

entracte *m* interval

entraînement *m* training

entre between

entrecôte *f* rib steak; **entrecôte Bercy** rib steak in butter, white wine and shallot sauce; **entrecôte chasseur** rib steak in sauce with shallots, white wine, tomato and mushrooms; **entrecôte grillée** grilled rib steak; **entrecôte marchand de vin** rib steak in red wine sauce with shallots

entrée *f* entry; entrance; admission; hall; starter *(food)*; **prix d'entrée** admission fee; **entrée gratuite** admission free; **entrée interdite** no entry

entremets *m* cream dessert

entrepreneur *m* contractor

entreprise *f* firm; company

entrer to come in; to go in

entretien *m* maintenance

enveloppe *f* envelope; **enveloppe autocollante** self-seal envelope; **enveloppe timbrée à votre adresse** stamped addressed envelope

envers *m* : **l'envers** wrong side; **à l'envers** upside down; back to front; inside out

environ around; about

environs *mpl* surroundings

envoi *m* dispatching; remittance; consignment; **envoi recommandé** registered post

épais(se) thick

épargne *f* saving

épaule *f* shoulder

éperlan *m* smelt *(fish)*

épi *m* ear *(of corn)*; **épi de maïs** corn-on-the-cob); **stationnement en épi** angled parking

épice *f* spice

épicé(e) spicy

épicerie *f* grocer's shop; **épicerie fine** delicatessen

épilation *f* : **épilation à la cire** hair

removal by waxing
épinards *mpl* spinach
épingle *f* pin
éponge *f* sponge
époque *f* age; **d'époque** period *(furniture)*
épreuve *f* event *(sports)*; print *(photographic)*
épuisé(e) sold out; out of stock
équipage *m* crew
équipe *f* team; shift
équipement *m* equipment; facilities
équitation *f* horse-riding
escale *f* stopover; call
escalier *m* stairs; **escalier roulant/mécanique** escalator; **escalier de secours** fire escape
escalope *f* escalope; **escalope viennoise/milanaise** veal escalope in breadcrumbs/in breadcrumbs and tomato sauce
escargot *m* snail
espace *m* space
espadon *m* swordfish
Espagne *f* Spain
espagnol(e) Spanish
espèce *f* sort; **en espèces** in cash
essai *m* trial; test
essayage *m* fitting *(dress)*
essence *f* petrol
essorer to spin(-dry); to wring
est[1] *m* east; **de l'est** eastern
est[2] see GRAMMAR
esthéticienne *f* beautician
esthétique *f* beauty salon
estivants *mpl* (summer) holiday-makers

estomac *m* stomach
estouffade *f* : **à l'estouffade** braised or steamed in very little cooking liquid
estragon *m* tarragon; **crème d'estragon** cream of tarragon (soup)
esturgeon *m* sturgeon
et and
étage *m* storey; **premier étage** 1st floor
étain *m* tin; pewter
étang *m* pond
étape *f* stage
état *m* state; **état des lieux** inventory of fixtures
été *m* summer
éteindre: éteignez turn off; **éteignez votre moteur** turn off your engine; **éteignez vos phares** turn off your headlights
êtes see GRAMMAR
étiquette *f* label; tag
étoile *f* star
étonnant(e) amazing
étouffée *f* : **à l'étouffée** braised
étranger(ère) *m/f* foreigner; **à l'étranger** overseas; abroad
étrennes *fpl* Christmas box
étroit(e) narrow; tight
étude *f* study; office; practice *(of lawyer)*
étudiant(e) *m/f* student
étuvée *f* : **à l'étuvée** braised
eux them
événement *m* occasion; event
excédent de bagages *m* excess bagage

excès *m* excess

exclusivité *f* exclusive rights

excursion *f* trip; outing; excursion; **excursion à pied** hiking

excuses *fpl* apologies

exemplaire *m* copy; **en double exemplaire** in duplicate

exigence *f* requirement

expéditeur *m* sender

expérimenté(e) experienced

expertise *f* valuation; assessment

exportation *f* export

exposition *f* exhibition

exprès on purpose; deliberately

express *m* espresso coffee; express train; **double express** large espresso

extérieur(e) outside

extincteur *m* fire extinguisher

extra top-quality; first-rate

extra-fin(e) extra fine; **bonbons/ chocolats extra-fins** superfine sweets/chocolates

extra-fort(e): moutarde extra-forte extra-strong mustard

extrait *m* extract

extra-sec very dry

fabrication *f* manufacturing; **de fabrication artisanale** craftsman-made

fabriqué: fabriqué en ... made in ...

face *f*: **en face (de)** opposite

façon *f* way; manner; **ne pas utiliser de façon prolongée** do not use over a prolonged period

facture *f* invoice

faïence *f* earthenware

faim *f* hunger

faire to make; to do; **faire signe au conducteur** signal to the driver to stop; **il fait chaud** it is hot; **faites le 4** dial 4

faisan *m* pheasant

fait(e): fait main handmade

famille *f* family

fantaisie *f* fancy

farce *f* farce; dressing; stuffing; **farces et attrapes** jokes and novelties

farci(e) stuffed

farine *f* flour; **farine lactée** baby cereal

fausse fake; false; wrong

fauteuil *m* armchair; seat *(at front of theatre)*

faux fake; wrong; false; **détecteur de faux billets** forged banknote detector

faux-filet *m* sirloin

félicitations *fpl* congratulations

femme *f* woman; wife; **femme de chambre** chambermaid; **femme de ménage** cleaner *(of house)*

fenêtre *f* window

fenouil *m* fennel

fente *f* crack, slot

fer *m* iron *(material, golf club)*

féra *f* freshwater fish *(Switz.)*

férié(e): jour férié public holiday

ferme[1] firm

ferme[2] *f* farmhouse; farm

fermé(e) shut

fermer to close; to shut; to turn off *(water)*; **fermer à clé** to lock

fermeture *f* closing

fermier *m* farmer

fermier(ière): poulet/beurre fermier farm chicken/butter

ferroviaire railway; rail

fête f holiday; fête; **fêtes (de fin d'année)** Christmas and New Year holidays

feu m fire; traffic lights; **feu d'artifice** fireworks; **feu de joie** bonfire; **feu rouge** red light; **au feu de bois** charcoal-grilled

feuille f sheet *(of paper)*

feuilleté m : **feuilleté aux escargots** pastry with snail filling

feutre m felt; felt-tip pen

feux mpl traffic lights; **feux de position** sidelights

fève f broad bean; charm in cake *(for Twelfth Night)*

février m February

fiche f slip *(of paper)*

fiche-horaire f train timetable

fièvre f fever

figue f fig

figure f face; figure

fil m thread; lead *(electrical)*; **fil électrique** wire; **fil de fer** wire

file f lane; row *(behind one another)*

filet m net; fillet *(of meat, fish)*; **filet à bagages** luggage rack; **filet mignon** small steak; **filet de sole aux amandes** fillet of sole with almonds; **filet de sole meunière** sole cooked in butter and served with lemon; **filets de perche** fried small fillets of perch

fille f daughter; **jeune fille** girl *(young woman)*

fillette f girl *(child)*

film m film; **film d'épouvante** horror

film

fils m son

fin f end; **fin d'interdiction de stationner** end of parking restrictions

fin(e) thin *(material)*; fine *(delicate)*

finale f finals *(sports)*

fine f liqueur brandy; **fine de claire** green oyster

fines herbes fpl mixed herbs

finir to end; to finish

flacon m bottle *(small)*

flamand(e) Flemish

flambé(e) flamed, usually with brandy

flan m custard tart; **flan aux cerises** cherry tart; **flan au roquefort** savoury tart with Roquefort cheese

flèche f arrow

fléché(e): itinéraire fléché route signposted with arrows

flétan m halibut

fleur f flower

fleuriste m/f florist

fleuve m river

flipper m pinball

flocon m flake; **flocons d'avoine** rolled oats

flûte f long, thin loaf

foie m liver; **foie gras** goose liver; **foie de volaille** chicken liver

foire f fair; **foire à/aux ...** special offer on ...

fois f time; **une fois** once

folle mad

foncé(e) dark *(colour)*

fonctionnement m : **en cas de non fonctionnement** in the event of a malfunction

fonctionner to work; **fonctionne sur secteur et sur piles** mains and battery operated

fond *m* back (of hall, room); bottom; **fond d'artichaut** artichoke heart

fonds *m* : **fonds de commerce** business

fondue *f* : **fondue (au fromage)** cheese fondue; **fondue bourguignonne/savoyarde** meat/gruyère cheese fondue; **fondue chinoise** thin slices of beef dipped into boiling stock and eaten with various sauces

forestière: à la forestière garnished with sautéed mushrooms, potatoes and bacon

forêt *f* forest

forfait *m* fixed price

forfaitaire: prix/indemnité forfaitaire inclusive price/payment

forme *f* form; shape; **en (bonne) forme** fit; **en bonne et due forme** duly

formel(le) positive (definite)

formulaire *m* form (document)

formule *f* formula; method; system; **selon la formule choisie** depending on the method chosen; **formule du tout compris** all-inclusive package

fou crazy (prices)

fouettée whipped (cream, eggs)

four *m* oven; **au four** baked

fourchette *f* fork

fournitures *fpl* supplies; **fournitures scolaires** school stationery

fourré(e) fur-lined (coat, boots); filled (pancake, chocolate, etc)

fourrière *f* pound (for animals, cars)

fourrure *f* fur

foyer *m* hostel; **foyer de jeunes** youth club

fraîche fresh; cool; wet (paint)

frais[1] fresh; cool

frais[2] *mpl* costs; expenses; **frais de réservation/d'annulation** booking/cancellation charges

fraise *f* strawberry

fraisier *m* sponge cake filled with strawberries and lemon cream

framboise *f* raspberry

français(e) French

frangipane *f* almond paste

frappé(e) iced (drink)

frein *m* brake

frère *m* brother

fret *m* freight (goods)

friand *m* sausage roll

friandises *fpl* sweets

fricandeau *m* : **fricandeau (de veau)** rolled, filled veal fillet

frigorifique refrigerating

frisé(e) curly

frisée *f* curly endive

frit(e) fried

frites *fpl* French fried potatoes; chips

friture *f* fried food; **friture de poissons** fried fish

froid(e) cold; **servir froid** to serve chilled

fromage *m* cheese; **fromage blanc (aux herbes)** soft white cheese (with herbs); **fromage fondu (pour tartines)/fromage à tartiner** cheese spread; **fromage frais** cream cheese; **fromage de tête** pork brawn

fromagerie f cheese dairy

froment m wheat

frontière f border; boundary

frotter to rub

fruit m fruit; **fruits de mer** shellfish (on menu); seafood; **fruit givré** fruit sorbet (served in skin of the fruit); **fruits confits** crystallized fruits; **fruits fourrés** stuffed fruit

fumer to smoke

fumeur m smoker

funiculaire m funicular railway

fuseau m ski pants; **fuseau horaire** time zone

gagnant(e) m/f winner

galantine f boned poultry/game, stuffed, cooked in a gelatine broth and served cold

galerie f art gallery (commercial); **galerie marchande/commerciale** arcade

galette f flat cake; **galette des rois** cake eaten on Twelfth Night

gambas fpl large prawns

gamme f range

gant m glove

garçon m boy; waiter

garde m guard (sentry); **pharmacie/ médecin de garde (la/le plus proche)** (nearest) duty chemist/doctor on duty

gardé(e): gardé/non gardé attended/ unattended; with/without resident warden

garderie d'enfants f crèche

gardez: gardez votre ticket sur vous keep your ticket; **gardez vos distances** keep your distance

gardien(ne) m/f caretaker; warden; **gardien de nuit** night porter

gare f railway station; **gare routière** bus terminal

garer to park

garni(e) served with vegetables; **garni(e) frites** served with chips; **hôtel garni** hotel serving breakfast only (Switz.)

garniture f accompanying vegetables

gas-oil m diesel fuel

gâteau m cake; gateau; **gâteau de riz** rice pudding; **gâteau sec** biscuit

gauche left; **à gauche** to/on the left

gaufre f waffle

gaufrette f wafer

gaz m gas

gazéifié(e) aerated

gazeux(euse) fizzy

gaz-oil m diesel fuel

gazole see **gaz-oil**

géant m giant

gel m frost

gelée f jelly; **poulet en gelée** chicken in aspic

gélule f capsule

gendarme m policeman

gendarmerie f police station

gêner: ne pas gêner la fermeture des portes do not obstruct the doors

généraliste m/f general practitioner

Genève Geneva

genièvre m juniper

génoise f sponge cake

gérant(e) *m/f* manager/manageress

Gewürztraminer *m* fruity, spicy, white wine from Alsace

gibelotte de lapin *f* rabbit stew with wine

gibier *m* game *(hunting)*

gigot (d'agneau) *m* leg of lamb

gilet *m* : **gilet de sauvetage** life jacket

gingembre *m* ginger

giratoire *see* **sens**

girolle *f* chanterelle mushroom

gîte *m* self-catering house/flat; **gîte rural** self-catering house/flat in the country; **gîte d'étape** dormitory accommodation

givré(e): mandarine/orange givrée mandarin/orange sorbet served in its skin

glace *f* ice; ice cream; mirror; **glace plombière** tutti frutti ice cream; **ouverture et fermeture des glaces** opening and closing of the windows

glacé(e) chilled; iced

glacier *m* glacier; ice-cream maker; ice-cream man

glaçon *m* ice cube

glissant(e) slippery; **chaussée glissante** slippery road surface

global(e) inclusive *(costs)*

gogo: à gogo galore

gorge *f* throat

goujon *m* gudgeon

gourmand(e) greedy

goût *m* flavour; taste

goûter[1] to taste

goûter[2] *m* afternoon tea

goutte *f* drip; drop

gracieusement free of charge

grain *m* : **café en grains** coffee beans; **poivre en grains** whole peppercorns

graine *f* seed; **graines de soja** soya beans

graissage *m* lubricating

grand(e) great; high *(speed, number)*; big

Grande-Bretagne *f* Great Britain

grande surface *f* hypermarket

grand marnier *m* orange liqueur

granité *m* water ice; **granité aux pommes** apple cake

gras(se) fat; greasy

gras-double *m* tripe

gratin *m* cheese-topped dish; **au gratin** with cheese topping; **gratin dauphinois** thinly-sliced potatoes baked with milk and cream and grated gruyère cheese

gratiné(e) with cheese topping; **gratinée au fromage** onion soup with grated cheese

gratis free

gratuit(e) free of charge

gravillon *m* grit; **projection de gravillons** loose chippings

gravure *f* print *(picture)*

grec (grecque) Greek; **à la grecque** in olive oil and herbs

grenadin *m* thick slice of veal fillet

grenadine *f* grenadine syrup

grenouille *f* frog

grève *f* strike *(industrial)*; **en grève** on strike

gribiche (in a) sauce made with hard-boiled egg yolks, oil and vinegar

grill *m* grillroom

grillade *f* grilled meat; **grillade feu de bois** charcoal-grilled meat

grille-pain *m* toaster

griotte *f* Morello cherry

gris(e) grey

gros(se) big *(sum of money)*; large; **en gros** in bulk; wholesale; **de gros** wholesale *(price)*; **gros lot** jackpot; **gros sel** cooking salt

groseille *f* redcurrant; **groseille à maquereau** gooseberry

grotte *f* cave

groupe *m* : **groupe sanguin** blood group

gruyère *m* hard Swiss cheese with delicate flavour

gué *m* ford

guichet *m* ticket office; **guichet automatique/libre-service** automatic cash dispenser

guide¹ *m* guidebook

guide² *m/f* guide

gymnase *m* gym(nasium); secondary school *(Switz. only)*

H = heure

habit *m* outfit; tails

habitant(e) *m/f* inhabitant

habituel(le) usual; regular

haché(e): steak haché hamburger

hachis *m* minced beef; **hachis Parmentier** cottage pie

halles *fpl* central food market

hareng *m* herring; **hareng salé/fumé** salt/smoked herring; **hareng saur** smoked herring

haricot *m* : **haricot de mouton** lamb or mutton stew

haricots *mpl* beans; **haricots blancs** haricot beans; **haricots mange-tout** runner beans; **haricots rouges** kidney beans; **haricots verts** green beans

haut *m* top *(of ladder)*; **vers le haut** upwards

haut(e) high; tall; **plus haut(e)** higher

hauteur *f* height; **hauteur limite** maximum height

hebdomadaire weekly

hébergement *m* lodging

herbe *f* : **fines herbes** herbs

herboristerie *f* herbalist's shop

heure *f* hour; **toutes les heures** hourly; **à toute heure** at any time; **heures de bureau** office hours; **heures d'ouverture/de fermeture** opening/closing times; **à l'heure** on time

heureux(euse) happy

hier yesterday

hippique: club hippique riding club

hippodrome *m* racecourse

hiver *m* winter

hollandais(e) Dutch; **sauce hollandaise** sauce made with butter, egg yolks and lemon juice

homard *m* lobster; **homard à l'américaine/l'armoricaine** lobster cooked in oil, with tomatoes, shallots and white wine; **homard à la nage** lobster cooked in stock made with vegetables and white wine or vinegar; **homard Thermidor** lobster in white wine, with mushrooms, spices, mustard, flamed with brandy

homme *m* man

hôpital *m* hospital

horaire *m* timetable *(for trains etc)*; schedule; **horaire des départs** departure board

horodateur(trice) *m/f* ticket machine ; **prendre un ticket à l'horodateur** get a ticket from the machine

hors: hors de out of; **hors service** out of order

hors d'oeuvre *m* starter

hors-saison off-season

hors-taxe duty-free

hôte *m* host; guest; **hôte payant** paying guest

hôtel *m* hotel

hôtel de ville *m* town hall

huile *f* oil *(edible, for car)*; **huile d'arachide** groundnut oil; **huile solaire** suntan oil; **huile de tournesol** sunflower oil

huit eight

huître *f* oyster; **huîtres portugaises** small, fat Atlantic oysters

humide damp; wet

hydromel *m* mead

hydrophile: coton hydrophile cotton wool

hygiaphone *m* **: parlez devant l'hygiaphone** please speak through the hygienic grill

hypermarché *m* hypermarket

ici here

il *m* he; it

île *f* island; **île flottante** caramelized beaten egg white poached in milk, with almonds and vanilla custard

illimité(e) unlimited

ils they

imbattable unbeatable

immeuble *m* block of flats

immobilier *m* real estate

impair(e) odd *(number)*

impasse *f* dead end

imperméable waterproof

impôt *m* tax

imprenable: vue imprenable sur ... open outlook over ...

imprimé *m* printed matter; **ne jetez/mettez dans cette boîte ni journaux ni imprimés** do not put newspapers or other printed matter through this letter box

imprimerie *f* printing works; printing

incassable unbreakable

incendie *m* fire

inclure to include; **du 6 au 12 inclus** from 6th to 12th inclusive

incroyable incredible

indépendant(e) independent; self-contained

indexé(e) index-linked

indicateur *m* guide; timetable; **indicateur de rues** street directory

indicatif *m* **: indicatif de département** dialling code

indicatif(ive): à titre indicatif for (your) information

indications *fpl* instructions; directions *(to a place)*

inférieur(e) inferior; lower

infirme disabled

infirmerie *f* infirmary

infirmière *f* nurse

informations *fpl* news; information

infraction *f* offence

infusion *f* herbal tea

inondation *f* flood

inox *m* stainless steel

inscription *f* enrolment

inscrire to write (down); to enrol; **s'inscrire (à)** to enrol (in); to join

instantané(e) instant

institut *m* institute; **institut de beauté** beauty salon

interdiction *f* : **interdiction de fumer** no smoking

interdit(e) forbidden; **interdit aux piétons** pedestrians prohibited; **interdit au public** authorized personnel only; **interdit du 1er au 15 du mois** (entry) forbidden from 1st to 15th of the month

intéressant(e) interesting

intérieur(e) interior; inside; inner; **à l'intérieur** inside; indoors

intérimaire temporary

intersection *f* junction (on road)

interurbain(e) long-distance (phone call)

introduire to introduce; to insert; **introduisez votre monnaie** insert money

inutile useless; unnecessary

invalide *m/f* disabled person

invité(e) *m/f* guest

irlandais(e) Irish

issue *f* : **issue de secours** emergency exit; **rue/voie sans issue** dead end; no through road

italien(ne) Italian

itinéraire *m* route; **itinéraire bison futé/flèches vertes** alternative route avoiding heavy traffic; **itinéraire touristique** scenic route

j' *see* **je**

jambon *m* ham; **jambon de Bayonne** smoked Bayonne ham; **jambon cru** smoked (raw) ham; **jambon cuit** cooked ham; **jambon à l'os** baked ham; **jambon de Paris** boiled ham

jambonneau *m* knuckle of ham

janvier *m* January

jardin *m* garden; **jardin d'acclimatation** zoological garden(s); **jardin d'enfants** kindergarten

jardinier *m* gardener

jardinière *f* : **jardinière (de légumes)** mixed vegetables

jarret *m* knuckle, shin (of veal, beef etc)

jaune yellow

je/j' I

jetable disposable

jetée *f* pier

jeter to throw; **à jeter** disposable

jeu *m* set (collection); pack (of cards); gambling; game

jeudi *m* Thursday

jeune young

jeunesse *f* youth

joaillier(ière) *m/f* jeweller

joindre to join; to enclose

joli(e) pretty

jour *m* day; **le jour de l'An** New Year's Day; **jour de fermeture ...** closed on ...

journal *m* newspaper

journée *f* day *(length of time)*

juif (juive) *f* Jewish

juillet *m* July

juin *m* June

julienne *f* vegetable consommé; vegetables cut into fine strips

jumelé(e): (ville) jumelée avec ... (town) twinned with ...

jupe *f* skirt

jus *m* juice; **au jus** in its own juice; **jus de citron** lemon juice; **jus de viande** gravy

jusqu'à until; till; **jusqu'à 6** up to 6

kart *m* go-cart

kas(c)her kosher

kayac *m* canoe

kermesse *f* fair; charity fête

kilométrage *m* ≈ mileage; **kilométrage illimité** unlimited mileage

kinésithérapeute *m/f* physiotherapist

kir *m* white wine with blackcurrant syrup

klaxonner to sound one's horn

kouglof/kugelhof *m* cake containing raisins, speciality of Alsace

l' *see* **le, la**

la/l' the; her; it

lac *m* lake

laine *f* wool; **de/en laine** woollen

laisse *f* leash; **tenez votre chien en laisse** keep your dog on a leash

laisser: laissez votre manteau ici leave your coat here; **laisser un message** leave a message

lait *m* milk; **lait caillé** junket; **lait chaud grande tasse** large hot milk; **lait concentré** condensed milk; **lait condensé (non sucré)** (unsweetened) evaporated milk; **lait démaquillant** cleansing milk; **lait demi-écrémé** semi-skimmed milk; **lait écrémé** skim(med) milk; **lait entier** full-cream milk; **lait maternisé** baby milk; **lait en poudre** dried milk; **lait de poule** eggflip

laitages *mpl* milk products

laiterie *f* dairy

laitue *f* lettuce

lame *f* blade

lampe *f* light; lamp

landau *m* pram

langouste *f* crayfish *(saltwater)*

langoustines *fpl* scampi

langue *f* tongue; language

lapereau *m* young rabbit

lapin *m* rabbit; **lapin chasseur** rabbit cooked in white wine and herbs

laque *f* hair spray

lard *m* fat; (streaky) bacon; **lard fumé** smoked bacon; **lard maigre** lean bacon

lardon *m* strip of fat

large wide; broad

largeur *f* width

laurier *m* bay leaves

lavable washable

lavabo *m* washbasin; **lavabos** toilets

lavage *m* washing

lavande *f* lavender

laverie automatique *f* launderette

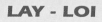

layette f baby clothes

le/l' the; him; it; **le jeudi** on Thursdays

leçon f lesson; **leçons particulières** private lessons

léger(ère) light (not heavy); weak (tea)

légumes mpl vegetables

lentement slowly

lentille f lens (of glasses)

lentilles fpl lentils

les the; them

lessive f soap powder; washing

lettre f letter; **lettre recommandée** registered letter

leur(s) them; their

levain m : **pain au levain** leavened bread

levée f collection (of mail)

lever du soleil m sunrise

levure f yeast

liaison f : **liaison hélicoptère/ ferroviaire** helicopter/rail link

libérer: la chambre devra être libérée le ... the room must be vacated on ...

librairie f bookshop

librairie-tabac-presse f bookseller's, tobacconist's and newsagent's

libre free; vacant

libre-service self-service

liégeois(e): café/chocolat liégeois coffee/chocolate ice cream with whipped cream

lieu¹ m place

lieu² m hake

lièvre m hare

ligne f line; service; route (transport); **grandes lignes** main lines (trains)

limande-sole f lemon sole

limitation de vitesse f speed limit

limonade f lemonade

lin m linen (cloth)

linge m linen (for bed, table); laundry (clothes); **linge de maison** household linen

liste f list; **liste d'attente** waiting list

lit m bed; **grand lit** double bed; **lit d'enfant** cot; **lit simple** single bed; **lits jumeaux** twin beds

livarot m pungent and spicy cow's milk cheese from Normandy

livraison f delivery (of goods); **livraison des bagages** baggage claim; **livraison à domicile** deliveries carried out

livre¹ f pound; **livre sterling** sterling

livre² m book

local m premises; **local à skis** ski room

locataire m/f tenant; lodger

location f rental; hiring (out); letting; **location à la journée/la semaine** daily/weekly hire (cars etc); **location à la semaine/au mois/à l'année** weekly/monthly/ annual lets (property); **location ouverte** booking office open; **location de voitures** car hire

location-vente f hire purchase

locaux mpl premises

logement m accommodation; housing

loger to accommodate; to stay

loi f law

loin far

loisir *m* leisure

Londres London

long(ue) long; **le long de** along

longe *f*: **longe de veau** loin of veal

longueur *f* length

loqueteau *m*: **maintenez le loqueteau levé** hold the handle up

lot *m* prize; lot *(at auction)*; **gros lot** jackpot

lotissement *m* plot *(of land)*

loto *m* numerical lottery

lotte *f* turbot; angler fish; **lotte à l'armoricaine/l'américaine** turbot/angler fish in sauce containing tomatoes, butter, cognac and white wine; **lotte au poivre vert** turbot/angler fish with green peppercorns

louer to let; to hire; to rent; **à louer** to let *(house etc)*

loukoum *m* Turkish delight

loup *m* bass *(fish)*

lourd(e) heavy

loyer *m* rent

luge *f* sledge; toboggan

lumière *f* light

lunch *m* buffet lunch

lundi *m* Monday

lune *f* moon

lunettes *fpl* glasses; **lunettes de soleil** sunglasses

luxe *m* luxury

luxueux(euse) luxurious

lycée *m* secondary school

lyonnaise: **à la lyonnaise** sautéed with onions

M sign for the Paris metro

m' *see* me

ma my

macédoine *f*: **macédoine de fruits** fruit salad; **macédoine de légumes** mixed vegetables

mâche *f* salad

Mâcon *m* good ordinary red and white wines

Madame *f* Mrs; Ms; Madam

madeleine *f* small sponge cake

Mademoiselle *f* Miss

madère *m* Madeira *(wine)*

magasin *m* shop

magnétophone *m* tape recorder

magnétoscope *m* video-cassette recorder

magret (de canard) *m* breast fillet of fattened duck

mai *m* May

maigre lean *(meat)*

maigrir to slim

maillot de bain *m* swimsuit

main *f* hand; **fait(e) à la main** handmade

maintenant now

maintenir: **maintenez le loqueteau levé** hold the handle up

mairie *f* town hall

maïs *m* maize; **maïs doux** sweet corn

maison *f* house; home; **à la maison** at home; **un gâteau maison** a home-made cake

maison-témoin *f* showhouse

maître d'hôtel *m* head waiter; **entrecôte maître d'hôtel** rib steak fried in butter with parsley and lemon juice

maître nageur sauveteur m swimming and life-saving instructor

majoration f increase; surcharge

majuscule f capital letter

mal badly; **mal aux dents** toothache; **le mal de mer** seasickness; **mal de tête** headache

malade m/f sick person; patient

maladie f disease

maman f mum(my)

Manche (la) the Channel

mandarine f tangerine

mandat m money order

mandat-carte m money order

mandat-lettre m money order (with space for message)

manger to eat

manifestation f demonstration

manque m shortage; lack; **par manque de ...** through lack of ...

manteau m coat

manucure m/f manicurist

maquereau m mackerel

maquillage m make-up

marais m swamp

marbre m marble (material)

marc m spirit distilled from residue of grapes

marcassin m young wild boar

marchand m dealer; merchant; **marchand de journaux** newsagent; **marchand de légumes** greengrocer; **marchand de vin** wine merchant; red wine sauce with shallots

marche f step; march; **attention à la marche** mind the step; **(en) marche** on (machine); **ne pas ouvrir en marche** do not open while the vehicle is in motion; **marche à pied** walking

marché m market; **marché aux puces** flea market; **bon marché** inexpensive

marcher to walk

mardi m Tuesday; **mardi gras** Shrove Tuesday

marécage m marsh

marée f tide; **marée basse** low tide; **marée haute** high tide

marengo: poulet/veau marengo chicken/veal cooked in white wine with tomatoes, garlic and mushrooms

marié m bridegroom

Marie-Brizard ® m aniseed-flavoured aperitif

mariée f bride

marinade f : **marinade de veau** marinaded veal

mariné(e) marinaded

marionnettes fpl puppets

marjolaine f marjoram

maroquinerie f fine leather goods

marque f make; brand (name)

marron m chestnut; **marrons glacés** chestnuts cooked in syrup and glazed

mars m March

mas m house or farm in the South of France

massepain m marzipan

matelote f : **matelote d'anguilles** stewed eels in red wine with onions

matériaux mpl : **matériaux de**

construction building materials

matériel *m* equipment; kit

matière *f* subject; material

matin *m* morning

mauvais(e) bad; wrong

maux *mpl* pains

maximum *m* : **au maximum** at the most; as much as possible

mazot *m* small chalet *(Switz.)*

mazout *m* oil *(for heating)*

me/m' me; myself

méchoui *m* barbecue (of whole roast sheep)

médaillon *m* thin, round slice of meat

médecin *m* doctor; **médecin généraliste** general practitioner, G.P.

médicament *m* medicine; drug

Médoc *m* principal red wine area of Bordeaux

meilleur(e) best; better

mélange *m* mixture; blend

même same

ménage *m* housework; **femme de ménage** cleaner

mensuel(le) monthly

menthe *f* mint; mint tea; **menthe à l'eau** peppermint cordial

menu *m* (set) menu; **menu à prix fixe** set price menu; **menu gastronomique** gourmet menu; **menu touristique** tourist/low price menu

mer *f* sea

mercerie *f* haberdashery

merci thank you

mercredi *m* Wednesday

mère *f* mother

merguez *f* spicy sausage

meringué(e): tarte au citron meringuée lemon meringue pie

merlan *m* whiting

mérou *m* grouper

merveilleux(euse) wonderful; marvellous

messe *f* mass *(church)*

messieurs *mpl* men; gentlemen('s toilets)

mesure *f* measurement; **par mesure d'hygiène** in the interests of hygiene

météo *f* weather forecast

métier *m* trade; occupation; craft

métro *m* underground railway

mettre to put; to put on; **ne vous mettez pas en situation irrégulière** do not contravene the regulations

meublé(e) furnished

meubles *mpl* furniture; **meubles rustiques/de style** rustic/period furniture

meunière: sole/limande meunière sole/lemon sole coated in flour and fried in butter with lemon juice and parsley

Meursault *m* dry white wine from Burgundy

mi-bas *mpl* knee socks

midi *m* midday; noon; **le Midi** the south of France

miel *m* honey

mieux better; best

milieu *m* middle

militaire military; soldier

mille thousand

millefeuille m cream/vanilla slice

mince slim; thin

mine f expression; mine (for coal etc)

mineur(e) under age; **interdit aux mineurs de moins de 18 ans** no admittance to anyone under 18 years of age; **interdit aux mineurs non accompagnés d'un adulte** no admission to children not accompanied by an adult

minimum: au minimum at the very least

ministère m ministry (government)

Minitel ® m view-data system

minuit m midnight

mirabelle f plum; plum brandy

miroir m mirror

mise à disposition (des véhicules) f (vehicles) ready for collection

mise en plis f set (for hair)

mistral m strong northerly wind, in Provence

mixte mixed

mobilier m furniture

mode f fashion; **à la mode** fashionable

mode d'emploi m directions for use

modique modest

moelle f marrow (beef etc)

moindre least

moins minus; less; **moins de** less than; **le moins** the least

mois m month

moitié f half; **à moitié** half

moka m coffee cream cake; mocha coffee; **crème moka** coffee cream

molle soft

momentané(e) momentary; brief

Monbazillac m sweet white and ordinary red wines from the Dordogne

monde m world; people

moniteur m instructor; coach

monitrice f instructress; coach

monnaie f currency; change (money); **faire de la monnaie** to get/give change; **rend/ne rend pas la monnaie** change/no change given

monnayeur m automatic change machine; **pour entrer mettez la somme indiquée sur le monnayeur** to enter place the amount indicated in the slot

Monsieur m Mr; **monsieur** sir; gentleman

monstre enormous

montagne f mountain

montant m amount (total); **montant à payer** amount payable

mont-blanc m : **mont-blanc à la Chantilly** chestnut cream dessert with whipped cream

monter to take up; to go up; to rise; **monter à bord de/dans** to board; **monter sur** to climb

montre f watch

moquette f wall-to-wall carpet(ing)

morceau m piece; bit; cut (of meat)

morilles fpl morel mushrooms

Mornay in a cheese sauce

mortel(le) fatal

morue f salt cod

mot m note (letter); word

motif m pattern

moto f motorbike

motoneige f snowbike

mou soft

mouche f fly

mouchoir m handkerchief;
mouchoir en papier paper hanky

mouillé(e) wet

moule f mussel; **moules marinières**
mussels cooked in their shells with
white wine, shallots and parsley

moulin m mill

moulu(e) ground

mousse f foam; mousse; **mousse de
foie de volaille** chicken liver
mousse; **mousse à raser** shaving
foam; **collant/bas mousse** stretch
tights/stockings

mousseux(euse) sparkling

moustique m mosquito

moutarde f mustard

mouton m sheep; lamb or mutton

moyennant: moyennant supplément
in return for a supplement

moyenne f average

Moyen-Orient m Middle East

muguet m lily of the valley

municipalité f borough

muni(e): muni(e) de supplied with;
in possession of

munster m strong cheese from
Alsace

mur m wall

mûr(e) mature; ripe

mûre f blackberry

muscade f nutmeg

muscadet m dry white wine from
the Loire

muscat m muscatel: a sweet
dessert wine

musculation f body-building

musée m museum; art gallery

mutuelle f mutual benefit
insurance company

myrtille f bilberry

n' see **ne**

nager to swim

naissance f birth

nappé(e) coated (with chocolate etc)

natation f swimming

nature plain, without seasoning or
sweetening; black, without sugar
(tea, coffee)

naturel(le) natural; **au naturel** plain,
without seasoning or sweetening

nautique: club nautique sailing
club; **sports nautiques** water sports

navarin (de mouton) m mutton
stew

navet m turnip

navette f shuttle (service)

navigation f sailing; **navigation de
plaisance** yachting

navire m ship

ne/n': ne pas ... do not ...

né(e) born

nécessaire m bag; kit

négociant m merchant

neige f snow; **(à la) neige** with
beaten egg-whites

nettoyage m cleaning; **nettoyage à
sec** dry-cleaning

neuf new

neuve new

névralgie f headache

niçois(e): salade niçoise lettuce with
tomatoes, hard-boiled eggs,

anchovies, black olives, green peppers; **à la niçoise** with garlic, olives, anchovies, onions and tomatoes

niveau m level; standard

noce f wedding

nocturne m late opening; **match en nocturne** floodlit fixture

Noël m Christmas

noir(e) black

noisette f hazelnut; **noisette d'agneau** small boneless slice of lamb

noix f walnut; **noix de cajou** cashew nut; **noix de coco** coconut; **noix de muscade** nutmeg; **noix de veau** type of veal steak

nom m name; **nom déposé** registered trademark; **nom de famille** surname; **nom de jeune fille** maiden name

nombre m number

non no; not

non-fumeur m non-smoker

non-prioritaire minor (road)

nord m north

normal(e) normal; standard (size); regular; **(essence) normale** = 2-star petrol (Switz.)

normande: à la normande usually cooked with shrimps, gudgeon, mushrooms and cream

nos our

notaire m solicitor

note f note; bill; memo

notice f note; directions; instructions; **notice explicative** explanatory leaflet

nouilles fpl noodles

nourrisson m (unweaned) infant

nourriture f food

nous we; us

nouveau new

nouveautés fpl fashions

Nouvel-An m New Year

nouvelle new

nouvelles fpl news

novembre m November

noyer m walnut

nu(e) naked; bare

nuit f night

numéro m number; act (at circus etc); issue (of magazine); **numéro d'appel** number being called; **numero d'immatriculation/ minéralogique** registration number (on car)

numéroté(e): place numérotée numbered seat

objectif m objective; lens (of camera)

objet m object; **objets de valeur** valuable items; **objets trouvés** lost property

obligatoire compulsory

obtention f**: pour l'obtention de ...** in order to obtain ...

occasion f occasion; bargain; **d'occasion** used; second-hand

occupé(e) engaged; busy; hired (taxi)

octobre m October

œuf m egg; **œuf à cheval** egg on top; **œuf à la coque** boiled egg; **œuf dur** hard-boiled egg; **œuf sur le/au plat** fried egg; **œuf poché** poached egg; **œufs brouillés** scrambled eggs; **œufs en gelée** lightly poached eggs served in gelatine; **œufs (durs) mimosa** stuffed eggs; **œufs à la neige** floating islands

office *m* : **office du tourisme** tourist office

offre *f* offer

oie *f* goose

oignon *m* onion

oiseau *m* bird

olive *f* olive

olivier *m* olive (tree); olive *(wood)*

omelette *f* omelette; **omelette baveuse** runny omelette; **omelette de la mère Poularde** omelette with potatoes; **omelette norvégienne** baked Alaska

onde *f* wave

ongle *m* nail *(on finger, toe)*

or *m* gold; **en or** gold(en)

orage *m* thunderstorm

orange *f* orange; **orange pressée** fresh orange drink

ordinaire ordinary; **(essence) ordinaire** = 2-star petrol

ordonnance *f* prescription

ordre *m* order; **à l'ordre de** payable to

ordures *fpl* rubbish

oreille *f* ear

orfèvre *m* goldsmith; silversmith

orgeat *m* : **sirop d'orgeat** barley water

Orient *m* the East

orienté(e): orienté(e) à l'est/au sud facing east/south

O.R.L. *m* ear, nose and throat

specialist

os *m* bone

oseille *f* sorrel

osier *m* wicker

ou or

où where

oui yes

oursin *m* sea urchin

ouvert(e) open; on *(water, gas etc)*; **ouvert sans interruption de 9h à 19h** open all day from 9 a.m. to 7 p.m.

ouverture *f* overture; opening; **ouverture prochaine** opening soon; **l'ouverture se fera automatiquement** it will open automatically

ouvrable working *(day)*

ouvrir to open; to turn on; to unlock

paiement *m* payment

paille *f* straw

pain *m* bread; loaf of bread; **petit pain** roll; **pain azyme** unleavened bread; **pain bis** brown bread; **pain de campagne** farmhouse bread; **pain au chocolat** croissant pastry with chocolate filling; **pain de chou-fleur/courgettes** cauliflower/courgette loaf; **pain complet** wholemeal bread; **pain d'épices** gingerbread; **pain grillé** toast; **pain au levain** leavened bread; **pain de mie** sandwich loaf; **pain de poisson** fish loaf; **pain aux raisins** currant bun; **pain de seigle** rye bread; **pain de son** bran bread

pair(e) even

paire *f* pair

palais *m* palace

palier *m* landing

palourde *f* clam

pamplemousse *m* grapefruit

panaché *m* shandy

panaché(e) mixed

pancarte *f* notice

pané(e) in breadcrumbs

panier *m* basket; **panier repas** packed lunch

panne *f* breakdown; **en panne** out of order

panneau *m* sign; **panneau indicateur** signpost

pantalon *m* trousers

papa *m* dad(dy)

papeterie *f* stationer's shop

papier *m* paper; **papiers** (identity) papers; (driving) licence; **papier d'aluminium** foil *(for food)*; **papier hygiénique** toilet paper

papillote *f*: **en papillote** wrapped in buttered paper and baked

Pâques *m* Easter

paquet *m* package; pack; packet

par by; through; per; **passer par Londres** to go via London; **deux fois par jour** twice a day; **par personne** per person

parapluie *m* umbrella

parc *m* park; **parc d'attractions** amusement park; **parc gardé** attended car-park; **parc de stationnement** car park

parcelle *f* plot *(of land)*

parcmètre *m* parking meter

parcours *m* distance; journey; route

pardon sorry; pardon?

pare-brise *m* windscreen

parent(e) *m/f* relative

parfait *m* ice cream dessert with fruit

parfait(e) perfect

parfum *m* perfume; flavour

parfumerie *f* perfume shop

pari *m* bet

parking *m* car-park; **parking couvert/découvert/souterrain** covered/open-air/underground car park; **parking surveillé/gardé** attended car park

parler to speak; to talk

Parmentier *see* **hachis**

paroisse *f* parish

partance *f*: **en partance** bound for

parterre *m* flowerbed

particulier(ière) private; particular

partie *f* part; round *(in competition)*

partir to leave; to go; **à partir de** from

pas[1] not; **pas de voitures** no cars

pas[2] *m* step; pace

passage *m* passage; **passage clouté** pedestrian crossing; **passage interdit** no through way; **passage à niveau** level crossing; **passage protégé** priority over secondary roads; **passage souterrain** underpass *(for pedestrians)*

passager(ère) *m/f* passenger

passé(e) past

passer to pass; to spend *(time)*; **se passer** to happen

passerelle *f* gangway *(bridge)*

passible: **passible d'amende/de prison** liable to a fine/imprisonment

passionnant(e) exciting

pastèque f watermelon

pasteur m minister (of religion)

pastis m aniseed-flavoured aperitif

pâte f pastry; dough; paste; batter; **pâte d'amandes** almond paste; **pâte dentifrice** toothpaste; **pâtes de fruits** crystallized fruit

pâté m pâté; **pâté de campagne** coarse-textured pâté usually made with pork; **pâté en croûte** pâté in a pastry crust

patère f peg (for coat)

pâtes fpl pasta

patin m skate; **patins à glace** ice skates; **patins à roulettes** roller skates

patinoire f skating rink

pâtisserie f cake shop; pastry (cake)

pâtissier-glacier m confectioner and ice-cream maker

patron m boss; pattern (dressmaking, knitting)

patronne f boss

paupiettes de veau fpl veal olives

pavé m : **pavé (de viande)** thick piece of steak

payant(e) who pay(s); which must be paid for

payé(e) paid; **payé(e) d'avance** prepaid

payer to pay (for)

pays m land; country; **du pays** local

paysage m scenery

Pays-Bas mpl Netherlands

péage m toll (on road etc)

peau f hide (leather); skin

pêche f peach; fishing; **pêche sous-marine/en mer** underwater/sea fishing

pêcheur m angler

pédicure m/f chiropodist

peignoir m dressing gown; bathrobe

peindre to paint; to decorate

peine f sorrow; bother (effort); **défense d'entrer sous peine d'amende/de poursuites** trespassers will be fined/prosecuted

peinture f paint

pellicule f film (for camera)

pelote f ball (of string, wool); **pelote basque** pelota (ball game for 2 players hitting a ball against a specially marked wall)

pelouse f lawn

pencher to lean; **se pencher** to lean over

pendant during

pendule f clock

penser to think

pension f : **demi-pension** half board; **pension complète** full board; **pension de famille** guest house; boarding house

pente f slope

Pentecôte f Whitsun

perche f perch

perdre to lose

perdreau m young partridge

perdrix f partridge

père m father; **père Noël** Santa Claus

périmé(e) out of date

période f period (of time)

périphérique m ring road

perle f bead; pearl

permanente f perm

permettre to permit (something)

permis m permit; **permis de conduire** driving licence

Pernod ® m aniseed-based aperitif

persil m parsley

persillade f oil, vinegar and parsley seasoning

perte f loss

pétanque f type of bowls played in the South of France

pet-de-nonne m fritter made with choux pastry

pétillant(e) fizzy

petit(e) small; slight; **petit déjeuner** breakfast; **petit pot** (jar of) baby food; **petit salé** salt pork; **petits pois** (garden) peas

petit-beurre m butter biscuit

petite friture f whitebait

petit-suisse m fresh unsalted double-cream cheese, eaten with sugar or fruit

pétrole m oil (petroleum); paraffin

peu little

peur f fear

peut-être perhaps

phare m headlight; lighthouse

pharmacie f chemist's (shop); pharmacy

photo d'identité f passport photo

photomaton m photo booth

pichet m jug

pièce f room (in house); coin; **pièce d'identité** (means of) identification; **pièce de rechange** spare part; **pièces détachées** spare parts

pied m foot; **à pied** on foot; **pieds de porc** pigs' trotters

pierre f stone

piéton m pedestrian

piétonnier(ère) pedestrianized

pigeonneau m young pigeon

pignon m pine kernel

pilaf m spicy rice cooked in stock to which mutton, chicken or fish is added

pile f pile; battery (for radio etc)

pilé(e) crushed; ground (almonds)

pilon m drumstick (of chicken)

pilule f pill

piment m chili

pincée f pinch (of salt etc)

pintade(au) f guinea fowl

pipérade f lightly scrambled eggs with tomato and peppers

piquante sauce made with white wine, vinegar, shallots, pickles and herbs

piqûre f bite (by insect); injection; sting

piscine f swimming pool; **piscine chauffée (de plein air)** (open-air) heated pool

pissaladière f onion tart with black olives, anchovies and sometimes tomatoes

pissenlit m dandelion

pistache f pistachio (nut)

piste f ski run; **piste cyclable** cycle track; **piste pour débutants** nursery slope; **piste de luge** toboggan run; **pistes tous niveaux** slopes for all levels of skiers

place f square (in town); seat; space (room); place; **sur place** on the spot; **places debout/assises** standing room/seats

placement *m* investment

plage *f* beach

plaisir *m* enjoyment; pleasure

plan *m* map *(of town)*; **plan d'eau** lake

planche *f*: **planche à voile** windsurfing

planeur *m* glider

plaque *f* plate *(of glass, metal)*; **plaque d'immatriculation/ minéralogique** number plate

plaqué(e) or/argent gold/silver-plated

plat *m* dish; course *(of meal)*; **plat du jour** dish of the day; **plat de résistance** main course; **plats à emporter** take-away meals; **plats préparés/cuisinés** ready-made meals/meals

plat(e) level *(surface)*; flat

plateau *m* tray; **plateau de fromages** assorted cheeses; **plateau de fruits de mer** seafood platter

plateau-repas *m* breakfast/lunch tray

plein(e) full; **plein(e) de** full of; **en/de plein air** open air; **plein sud** facing south

pliant *m* folding chair

plomb *m* lead; **essence sans plomb** unleaded petrol

plombier *m* plumber

plombières *f* tutti-frutti ice cream with whipped cream

plongée *f*: **plongée sous-marine** (skin) diving

plonger to dive

pluie *f* rain

plus more; most; **en plus** extra

pneu *m* tyre

poche *f* pocket

poché(e) poached

poêlé(e) fried

poids *m* weight; **poids lourd** heavy goods vehicle

poil *m* hair; coat *(of animal)*

poinçonner to punch *(ticket etc)*

point *m* stitch; dot; **à point** medium *(steak)*; **point de rassemblement** assembly point; **point de rencontre** meeting point; **point de vente** sales outlet; **point phone** coin-operated phone found in hotels and bars

pointe *f* point *(tip)*

pointillé: **suivant le pointillé** along the dotted line

pointure *f* size *(of shoes)*

poire *f* pear; pear brandy; **poire belle Hélène** poached pear served with vanilla ice cream and hot chocolate sauce

poireau *m* leek

pois *m* spot *(dot)*; **petits pois** peas; **pois cassés** split peas; **pois chiches** chick peas

poisson *m* fish; **poisson rouge** goldfish

poissonnerie *f* fishmonger's shop

poitrine *f* breast; chest

poivrade: **à la poivrade** in vinaigrette sauce with pepper; in white wine sauce with pepper

poivre *m* pepper

poivré(e) peppery

poivron *m* pepper *(capsicum)*; **poivron vert/rouge** green/red pepper

poli(e) polite

police f policy (insurance); police; **police secours** emergency services

policier m policeman; detective film/novel

pomme f apple; potato; **pommes à l'anglaise** boiled potatoes; **pommes dauphine** potatoes mashed with butter, egg yolks and flour, deep-fried as croquettes; **pommes duchesse** potatoes mashed with butter and egg yolks; **pommes (au) four** baked potatoes; **pommes frites** chips; **pommes gratinées** potatoes with cheese topping; **pommes à l'huile** fried potatoes; **pommes mousseline** mashed potatoes; **pommes noisette** deep fried potato balls; **pommes paille** potatoes sliced like straws and fried; **pommes sautées** sauté potatoes; **pommes vapeur** boiled potatoes

pomme de terre f potato; **pommes de terre au lard** potatoes with bacon; **pommes de terre en robe des champs** jacket potatoes

pommier m apple tree

pompes funèbres fpl undertaker's

pompier m fireman

pont m bridge; deck (of ship); extended weekend; **pont à péage** toll bridge

pont-l'évêque m softish, mature, square-shaped cheese

porc m pork; pig

porcelet m piglet

port m harbour; port; **port de plaisance** yachting harbour

portatif(ive) portable

porte f door; gate

portée f : **à votre portée** within your means

porteur m porter

portier m doorman

portillon m : **portillon automatique** automatic barrier

portion f helping; portion

porto m port (wine)

port-salut m mild, firm cow's milk cheese

poser to put; to lay down

posologie f dosage

posséder to own

poste[1] m (radio/TV) set; extension (phone); **poste de contrôle** checkpoint; **poste de secours** first-aid post

poste[2] f post; **service des postes** Post Office

pot m pot (for jam, for plant); carton (of yoghurt etc)

potable: eau potable drinking water

potage m soup; **potage à l'oseille** sorrel soup; **potage Saint-Germain** split-pea soup served with croutons

pot-au-feu m beef stew

poteau m post (pole); **poteau indicateur** signpost

potée f hotpot (of pork or beef with vegetables)

potiron m pumpkin

poubelle f dustbin

poudre f powder

Pouilly-Fuissé m light, dry white wine from Burgundy

Pouilly-Fumé m spicy, dry white wine from the Loire

poularde f fattened chicken

poule f hen; **poule en daube** chicken casserole; **poule au pot** stewed chicken with vegetables

poulet m chicken; **poulet basquaise** chicken pieces cooked with tomatoes, peppers, mushrooms, ham and wine; **poulet chasseur** chicken in sauce of wine, mushrooms, tomatoes and herbs; **poulet en cocotte** chicken casserole; **poulet frites** chicken with chips; **poulet rôti** roast chicken

poulette: sauce poulette sauce made with white stock, lemon juice, wine, parsley and sometimes mushrooms

pourboire m tip

pourquoi why

pousse-café m (after-dinner) liqueur

pousser to push

pousses de soja fpl beansprouts

poussez push

pouvoir to be able

praire f clam

praline f sugared almond

praliné(e) sugared; almond-flavoured

précédent(e) previous

préfecture de police f police headquarters

premier(ère) first; **de premier ordre** high-class; **voyager en première** to travel first class; **premiers secours** first aid

prendre to take; to get; to have (meal, shower, drink)

prénom m first name

près (de) near; **tout près** close by

pré-salé m salt meadow lamb

présélection f: **respecter la présélection** keep in lane

présenter to present (give); to introduce (person); **se présenter à l'enregistrement** to check in (at airport); **présenter une pièce d'identité** to show some identification

presqu'île f peninsula

pressé(e): orange/citron pressé(e) fresh orange/lemon drink

pressing m dry cleaner's

pression f pressure; **(bière à la) pression** draught beer; **faites vérifier la pression de vos pneus** have your tyre pressure checked

prestations fpl service (in hotel etc)

prêt(e) ready; **prêt à cuire** ready to cook

prêt-à-porter m ready-to-wear

prévision f forecast

prière f prayer; **prière de ...** please ...

primeurs fpl early fruit and vegetables

printemps m spring

prioritaire with right of way

priorité f right of way; **cédez la priorité** give way; **réservé en/par priorité à** strictly reserved for; **priorité à droite** give way to traffic coming from the right

prise f: **prise (de courant)** f plug; socket; **prise en charge** hire charge (rented car); pick-up charge (taxi)

privatif(ive) private

privé(e) private

prix m price; prize; **à prix réduit**

cut-price; **prix du billet** fare; **prix choc** drastic reductions; **prix de la course/du parcours** fare *(in taxi)*; **prix coûtant** cost price; **prix d'entrée** entrance fee; **prix imbattables** unbeatable prices; **prix sacrifiés** giveaway prices

prochain(e) next

proche close *(near)*

produits *mpl* produce; products; **produits d'entretien** cleaning products

profiter de to take advantage of

profiteroles *fpl* small cases of choux pastry with a sweet filling

profond(e) deep

profondeur *f* depth

promenade *f* walk; promenade; ride *(in vehicle)*; **promenades pédestres** rambles

promoteur (immobilier) *m* property developer

promotion *f*: **promotion sur ...** special offer on ...

promotionnel(le) special low-price

propre clean; own

propreté *f* cleanliness; tidiness; **en parfait état de propreté** perfectly clean (and tidy)

propriétaire *m/f* owner

propriété *f* property

provenance *f*: **en provenance de** from

provençal(e): **à la provençale** cooked in olive oil, with tomatoes, garlic and parsley

provisions *fpl* groceries

provisoirement for the time being

proximité *f*: **à proximité** nearby

prudence *f*: **prudence!** drive carefully!; **par mesure de prudence** as a precaution

prune *f* plum; plum brandy

pruneau *m* prune; damson *(Switz.)*; **pruneau sec** prune *(Switz.)*

prunelle *f* sloe; sloe gin

P.T.T. *fpl* Post Office

Publiphone à carte *m* cardphone

puce *f* flea; **(marché aux) puces** flea market

puissance *f* power

puissant(e) powerful

puits *m* well *(for water)*

pull *m* sweater

pure: **pure laine vierge** pure new wool

purée *f* purée; **purée de pommes de terre** mashed potatoes

P.V. *m* parking ticket

quai *m* platform *(in station)*; wharf; quay

quand when

quarantaine *f* about forty; quarantine

quart *m* quarter

quartier *m* neighbourhood; district

quatre four

quatre-quarts *m* pound cake

que that; than; whom; what

quel(le) which; what

quelque some

quelque chose something

quelqu'un someone

quenelle *f* light fish, poultry or meat dumpling

quetsche f damson; damson brandy

queue f queue; tail; **queues de langouste/langoustine** lobster/scampi tails

qui who; which

quincaillerie f hardware

quinquina m : **(apéritif au) quinquina** quinine tonic wine

quinzaine f about fifteen; a fortnight

quotidien(ne) daily

rabais m reduction; **3% de rabais** 3% off

rabat m flap

râble m : **râble de lapin/lièvre** saddle of rabbit/hare

raccrocher to hang up (phone); **raccrochez** hang up

raclette f hot, melted cheese served with boiled potatoes and pickles

radis m radish

raffiné(e) refined

rafraîchi(e): fruits rafraîchis fruit salad

rafraîchissements mpl refreshments

rage f rabies

ragoût m stew; casserole

raie f skate (fish); **raie au beurre noir** skate in brown butter sauce

raifort m horseradish

rainurage m rutted road surface

raisin m grape; **raisin sec** sultana; raisin; **raisins de mars** redcurrants (Switz. only)

raison f reason; **pour raison de santé** for health reasons

ralentir to slow down

rame f oar; train

ramequin m ramekin, individual soufflé dish

randonnée f hike; **faire une randonnée** to go for a hike; **chemins de grande randonnée** hiking routes; **randonnée pédestre** ramble

rapatriement m repatriation

râpé(e) grated

rapide[1] quick; fast

rapide[2] m express train

rappel m reminder

raquette f racket (tennis); bat (table tennis etc); snowshoe

rare rare; unusual

rascasse f scorpion fish

rasoir m razor; **rasoir électrique** shaver

ratatouille (niçoise) f aubergines, peppers, courgettes and tomatoes cooked in olive oil

R.A.T.P. f Paris transport authority

rayon m shelf; department (in store); **rayon hommes** menswear (department)

R. de C./R.C. see **rez-de-chaussée**

reboucher: reboucher le flacon après usage recork the bottle after use

récépissé m receipt

récepteur m receiver (phone)

recette f recipe

recharge f refill

rechargeable refillable (lighter, pen)

récipient m container

réclamation f complaint

réclame f advertisement; **en réclame** on offer

recommandé(e): (envoi) en recommandé registered mail

récompense f reward

reçu m receipt

récupérer to get back

réduction f: **carte de réduction** card entitling holder to a discount

réduire: réduit de moitié reduced by half

refroidir to cool (down); to get cold

refuge m mountain hut

refuser to reject; to refuse

régime m diet (slimming); **aliments de régime** health food

réglable adjustable; payable

règle f: **en règle** in order

règlement m regulation; payment; **règlement par chèque** payment by cheque; **règlement en espèces/au comptant** payment in cash

régler: à régler sur place to be paid at time of purchase/booking etc

réglisse f liquorice

reine f queen

reine-claude f greengage

relâche m: **relâche mardi** closed on Tuesdays

relais routier m transport café (good, inexpensive food)

religieuse f nun; cream bun (made with choux pastry)

remboursement m refund; **appuyez sur le bouton de remboursement** press the button to get your money back

rembourser to pay back; to refund

remède m remedy

remerciements mpl thanks

remercier to thank

remise m discount; **remise en état** repair; restoration

remontée mécanique f ski lift

remonte-pente m ski lift

remorquer to tow

rémoulade f mayonnaise with onions, capers, gherkins and herbs

remplir to fill; to fill in/out/up; **remplir une fiche d'hôtel** to check in (at hotel)

rencontrer to meet

rendez-vous m date; appointment; **sur rendez-vous** by appointment

rendre: cet appareil rend/ne rend pas la monnaie change given/no change given at this machine

renouveler to renew

renouvellement m renewal; replenishment

renseignements mpl information; directory enquiries; **pour tous renseignements (complémentaires)** for any (further) information

rentrée f return to work after the summer break; **rentrée (des classes)** start of the new school year

réparations fpl repairs

repas m meal; **repas à la place** meal served in your compartment

repassage m ironing

répertoire m list; **répertoire des rues** street index

répondre to reply; to answer

réponse f answer; reply

repos m rest

reprendre: reprenez votre ticket remove your ticket

représentation f performance (of play)

reprise f trade-in; repeat (film)

requis(e) required

R.E.R. m Greater Paris high-speed commuter train

réseau m network

réservation f reservation; booking

réserve f **: réserve de chasse/pêche** hunting/fishing preserve; **réserve naturelle** nature reserve

ressemelage m (re)soling

ressortissant(e) m/f national

restauroute see restoroute

rester to remain; to stay

restoroute m roadside or motorway restaurant

retard m delay; **en retard** late

retenir to reserve (seat etc); **retenez le numéro de votre file** remember your row number

retirer to withdraw; to collect (tickets)

retouche f: **(tous travaux de) retouche** alterations done

retour m return (going/coming back); **par retour (du courrier)** by return (of post)

retrait m withdrawal; collection; **en cas de non-retrait** in the event of failure to collect (tickets); **retrait d'espèces** cash withdrawal

retraité(e) m/f old-age-pensioner

réunion f meeting

réveil m alarm clock

réveillon m **: réveillon (de Noël/de la Saint-Sylvestre)** Christmas/New Year's Eve (party)

revoir: au revoir goodbye

rez-de-chaussée m ground floor

rhum m rum

rhumerie f bar specialising in rum-based drinks

riche rich

rien nothing; anything

rillettes fpl potted meat made from pork or goose; **rillettes de saumon** potted salmon

ris de veau m calf sweetbread

rissolé(e): pommes (de terre) rissolées fried potatoes

riverains m **: sauf riverains** no entry except for access; residents only; **stationnement réservé aux riverains** parking for residents only

rivière f river

riz m rice; **riz au lait** rice pudding; **riz pilaf** pilau rice

R.N. see route

robe f gown; dress

robinet m tap

rocade f ringroad

rocher m rock (boulder)

roesti mpl potato slivers fried with onion and bacon (Switz.)

rognon m kidney (to eat); **rognons sautés au madère** sautéed kidneys in madeira sauce

roi m king; **les rois/la fête des rois** Twelfth Night

romaine f cos lettuce

roman m novel

Romandie f French speaking Switzerland

romarin *m* rosemary

romsteak *m* rump steak

rond *m* ring *(circle)*

rond(e) round

rond-point *m* roundabout

roquefort *m* rich, pungent blue-veined cheese made from ewe's milk

rosbif *m* roast beef; roasting beef

rose pink

Rosé d'Anjou *m* light fruity rosé wine from the Loire

rôti *m* roast meat; joint

rôtie *f* slice of toast

rotin *m* rattan (cane)

rôtisserie *f* steakhouse; roast meat counter

rôtissoire *f* roasting spit

roue *f* wheel

rouelle de veau *f* shank of veal

rouge red

rouget *m* mullet

rouille *f* spicy Provençal sauce accompanying fish

roulade *f* rolled meat or fish with stuffing

roulé *m* Swiss roll

rouleau *m* roll; roller

rouler to roll; to go *(by car)*; **roulez lentement** drive slowly

route *f* road; route; **route barrée** road closed; **route nationale (R.N.)** trunk-road; **route à quatre voies** dual carriageway

routier *m* lorry driver

Royaume-Uni *m* United Kingdom

rue *f* street; **grande rue** high street

ruelle *f* lane *(in town)*; alley

rumsteck *m* rump steak

russe Russian

rutabaga *m* swede

S.A. Ltd; plc

sabayon *m* dessert of egg yolks, sugar and white wine, served warm

sable *m* sand; **de sable** sandy *(beach)*; **sables mouvants** quicksand

sablé *m* shortbread

sac *m* bag; **sac à dos** rucksack

sachet *m* sachet; **sachet de thé** tea bag

safran *m* saffron

sage good *(well-behaved)*; wise

saignant(e) rare *(steak)*

saint(e)[1] holy

saint(e)[2] *m/f* saint

Saint-Emilion *m* good full-bodied red wine from Bordeaux

saint-honoré *m* gateau decorated with whipped cream and choux pastry balls

saint-nectaire *m* firm, fruity-flavoured cow's-milk cheese from the Auvergne

saint-paulin *m* mild cow's-milk cheese

Saint-Sylvestre *f* New Year's Eve

saison *f* season; **haute/basse saison** high/low season

salade *f* lettuce; salad; **en salade** in vinaigrette; **salade campagnarde** green salad with chicken and diced cheese; **salade composée** salad dish; **salade de fruits** fruit salad; **salade lyonnaise** potato salad with sausage and gherkins; **salade**

de pommes de terre cold boiled potatoes in vinaigrette; **salade niçoise** mixed salad with French beans, tomatoes, peppers, potatoes, olives and anchovies

salaisons *fpl* salt meats

sale dirty

salé *m* salt pork

salé(e) salty; savoury

salle *f* lounge *(at airport)*; hall *(room)*; auditorium; **salle d'attente** waiting room; **salle de bains** bathroom; **salle d'eau** shower room; **salle à manger** dining room; **salle de séjour** living room

salmis *m* ragout of game stewed in a rich sauce of wine and vegetables

salon *m* sitting room; lounge; **salon de l'automobile** motor show; **salon de coiffure** hairdressing salon; **salon de thé** tea-shop

samedi *m* Saturday

S.A.M.U. *m* emergency medical service

Sancerre *m* dry white wine from the Loire

sanglier *m* wild boar

sanguine *f* blood orange

sans without; **sans issue** no through road

santé *f* health; **à votre santé!** cheers!; **en bonne santé** healthy

santon (de Provence) *m* figure for Christmas crib

sapeurs-pompiers *mpl* fire brigade

sapin *m* fir (tree); **sapin de Noël** Christmas tree

sarcelle *f* teal; small freshwater duck

S.A.R.L. *f* limited company

sarrasin *m* buckwheat

sarriette *f* savory

sauce *f* sauce

saucisse *f* sausage; **saucisse de Francfort** Frankfurter

saucisson *m* slicing sausage; **saucisson à l'ail** garlic sausage; **saucisson sec** (dry) pork and beef sausage

sauf except (for)

sauge *f* sage *(herb)*

saumon *m* salmon; **saumon fumé (d'Ecosse)** (Scottish) smoked salmon

sauté *m* : **sauté de poulet/mouton/ veau** chicken/mutton/veal lightly browned in hot butter, oil or fat

Sauternes *m* sweet white wine from Bordeaux

sauvage wild

sauvetage *m* rescue

sauvette *f* : **revendeur à la sauvette** street peddler

savarin *m* ring-shaped cake, soaked in syrup and a liqueur or spirit

savon *m* soap; **savon de Marseille** household soap

savonnette *f* bar of soap

scarole *f* endive

Schweppes ® *m* tonic water

scolaire school

scotch *m* Sellotape ®; whisky

séance *f* meeting; performance

sec (sèche) dried *(fruit, beans)*

sèche-cheveux *m* hairdryer

secouer to shake

secourisme *m* first aid

secours *m* help

secrétariat *m* office

secteur *m* sector; mains

sécurité *f* security; safety; **en sécurité** safe; **pour votre sécurité** for your safety; **sécurité routière** road safety

séduisant(e) seductive; attractive; glamorous

seigle *m* rye

séjour *m* stay; visit; **séjour en demi-pension** half board terms; **séjour en pension complète** full board terms

sel *m* salt; **sans sel** unsalted

self *m* self-service restaurant

semaine *f* week; **semaine commerciale** trade week

semoule *f* semolina

sens *m* meaning; direction; **sens giratoire** roundabout; **sens interdit** no entry; **sens unique** one-way street

sentier *m* footpath; **sentier de grande randonnée** ramblers' path

sept seven

septembre *m* September

série *f* series; set; **fins de série** oddments

SERNAM *m* rail delivery service (≈ *Red Star*)

serrer to grip; to squeeze; **véhicules lents serrez à droite** slow-moving vehicles keep to the right-hand lane

serrurerie *f* locksmith's

serveur *m* waiter; barman

serveuse *f* waitress; barmaid

servez-vous help yourself

service *m* service; service charge;

sauf service no entry except for access; staff only; **service après-vente** after-sales service; **service compris/non compris (s.n.c.)** service included/not included; **service médical d'urgence** emergency medical service

serviette *f* towel; serviette; briefcase

servir to dish up; to serve

seul(e) alone; lonely; **un seul** only one

seulement only

si if; whether; yes *(to negative question)*

siècle *m* century

siège *m* seat; head office; **siège social** registered office

sien: le sien his; hers

signal *m* signal; **le signal sonore annonce la fermeture des portes** the acoustic signal warns that the doors are about to close; **dès que le signal sonore fonctionne** when you hear the signal

signaler to report

signalisation *f*: **panneau de signalisation** roadsign; **feux de signalisation** traffic lights; **signalisation automatique** automatic signalling

signer to sign

s'il vous plaît please

simple simple; single

sirop *m* syrup

site *m* site; **site touristique** tourist spot

situé(e) located

six six

skaï ® *m* leatherette

ski *m* ski; skiing; **ski alpin/de piste** Alpine skiing; **ski de fond** langlauf; **ski hors piste/poudreuse** off-piste skiing; **ski nautique** water-skiing; **ski de randonnée** cross-country skiing

slip *m* underpants; panties; **slip de bain** swimming trunks

snack *m* snack bar

s.n.c. *see* service

S.N.C.F. *f* French railways

société *f* company; society

soda *m* fizzy drink

sœur *f* sister

soie *f* silk

soif *f* thirst

soin *m* care; **aux bons soins de** care of (c/o)

soir *m* evening; **le soir** in the evening; **ce soir** tonight

soirée *f* evening; party

soja *m* soya; soya beans; **germes de soja** beansprouts

sol *m* ground; soil

solde *m* balance *(remainder owed)*

soldes *mpl* sales *(cheap prices)*; **les soldes ne sont ni repris ni échangés** no exchange or refund on sale goods; **soldes de fins de série** oddments sale; **soldes permanents** sale prices all year round

sole *f* sole *(fish)*; **sole meunière** sole cooked in butter and served with lemon; **sole normande** sole in a sauce of white wine and cream

soleil *m* sun; sunshine

sommeil *m* sleep

sommelier *m* wine waiter

sommelière *f* barmaid *(Switz.)*

sonner to ring; to strike

sonnerie *f* bell *(electric)*

sonnette *f* bell *(on door)*

sonnez ring

sorbet *m* water ice

sortie *f* exit; **sortie de camions** heavy plant crossing; **sortie interdite** no exit; **sortie de secours** emergency exit

S.O.S. médecins *m* emergency doctor service

souhaiter: nous vous souhaitons ... we wish you ...

soulever to lift

soupe *f* soup; **soupe au chou** cabbage soup; **soupe à l'oignon (gratinée)** (French) onion soup; **soupe au pistou** thick soup from Provence, with beans, potatoes, courgettes, garlic and basil

souper *m* supper; dinner *(Switz.)*

sourd(e) deaf

sous underneath; under

souscrire: souscrire une assurance to take out an insurance policy

sous-sol *m* basement; **en sous-sol** underground

sous-vêtements *mpl* underwear; underclothes

souterrain(e) underground

spectacle *m* scene *(sight)*; show *(in theatre)*; entertainment

spectateurs *mpl* audience *(in theatre)*

spiritueux *mpl* spirits

sport *m* **: sports d'hiver** winter sports

sportif(ive) sports; athletic

S.S. (sous-sol) basement

stade *m* stadium

stage *m* training period; training course

standard *m* switchboard

standardiste *m/f* switchboard operator

station *f* station; **station balnéaire** seaside resort; **station climatique** health resort; **station d'essence** filling station; **station de taxis** taxi rank; **station thermale** spa

stationnement *m* parking; **stationnement alterné** parking on alternate sides depending on date; **stationnement gênant** no parking; **stationnement interdit/réglementé** no/restricted parking; **stationnement interdit en dehors des parcs** parking in car parks only; **stationnement limité à l'heure** parking limited to one hour

steak *m* : **steak frites** steak and chips; **steak au poivre** steak with peppercorns; **steak tartare** minced raw steak mixed with raw egg, onion, tartar sauce, parsley and capers

stylo *m* pen; fountain pen

succursale *f* branch *(of store, bank etc)*

sucette *f* lollipop

sucre *m* sugar; **sucre cristallisé/raffiné** coarse-grained/refined sugar; **sucre glace** icing sugar; **sucre en morceaux** lump sugar; **sucre roux** brown sugar; **sucre semoule** granulated sugar

sucré(e) sweet

sud *m* south

suisse Swiss

Suisse *f* Switzerland; **Suisse romande** French-speaking Switzerland; **Suisse allemande/alémanique** German-speaking Switzerland

suite *f* series; continuation

suivant(e) following

suivre to follow; **faire suivre** please forward *(letter)*

super(carburant) *m* four-star petrol

supérette *f* mini-market

supérieur(e) upper; higher; superior *(quality)*

supplément *m* : **vin en supplément** wine extra; **sans supplément (de prix)** no extra charge

supplémentaire extra

suprême *m* : **suprême de volaille** chicken breast in creamy sauce; **sauce suprême** sauce made with white stock, wine and cream

sur on; onto; on top of; upon; **3 mètres sur 5** 3 metres by 5

sûreté *f* : **pour plus de sûreté** as an extra precaution

surgelés *mpl* frozen foods

surveillant(e) *m/f* supervisor; **surveillant de plage** lifeguard

surveillé(e) supervised

surveillez vos bagages keep an eye on your luggage

sus: en sus in addition

Suze ® *f* gentian-based liqueur

s.v.p. please

Sylvaner *m* dry white wine from Alsace

sympa(thique) nice; pleasant

syndicat d'initiative *m* tourist office

t' *see* **te**

ta your *(familiar form)*

tabac *m* tobacco; tobacconist's *(shop)*

table *f* table; **table d'hôte** fixed-price menu

tableau *m* painting; picture; **tableau des départs/arrivées** departures/arrivals board

tablette de chocolat *f* bar of chocolate

taboulé *m* steamed semolina served cold with tomato, cucumber, olive oil, lemon juice

taille *f* height *(of person)*; size *(of clothes)*; waist; **grande taille** outsize *(clothes)*; **taille unique** one size

tailleur *m* tailor; suit *(women's)*

talon *m* heel; stub *(counterfoil)*; **talon minute** shoes heeled while you wait

tante *f* aunt(ie)

tapez dial

tapis *m* carpet

tard late; **au plus tard** at the latest

tarif *m* rate; tariff; **tarif des consommations** drinks tariff

tarte *f* flan; tart; **tarte au citron meringuée** lemon meringue pie; **tarte au fromage** cheese tart; **tarte aux mirabelles/aux raisins** plum/grape open tart; **tarte Tatin** upside-down tart of caramelized apples, served hot

tartelette *f* (small) tart

tartine *f* slice of bread and butter (or jam); **tartine beurrée** slice of bread and butter

tartiner: à tartiner for spreading

tasse *f* cup; mug

taux *m* rate; **taux du change** exchange rate; **taux fixe** flat rate

taxe *f* duty; tax *(on goods)*; **toutes taxes comprises (t.t.c.)** inclusive of tax; **taxe de séjour** tourist tax

T.C.F. = Touring Club de France *(automobile association)*

te/t' you *(familiar form)*

teint *m* complexion

teinturerie *f* dry cleaner's

télé *f* TV

télébenne *f* gondola lift

télécabine *f* gondola lift

télécarte *f* phonecard

téléphérique *m* cableway; cable-car

téléphone *m* : **téléphone avec ligne directe** telephone with direct outside line

télésiège *m* chair-lift

téléski *m* ski tow

téléviseur *m* television *(set)*

tempête *f* storm

temps *m* weather; time

tendre tender

tendron de veau *m* breast of veal

tenir to hold; to keep; **tenir la main courante** hold on to the handrail; **tenez votre doite** keep to the right

tennis *m* tennis; **les tennis** gym shoes

tension *f* voltage

tente *f* tent

tenue *f* clothes; dress; **tenue correcte/habillée exigée** lounge suits must be worn; **tenue de soirée** evening dress

tergal ® *m* Terylene ®

terrain *m* ground; land; field *(for football etc)*; course *(for golf)*; **terrain de camping** camping site

terrasse *f* terrace

terre *f* land; earth; ground

terrine *f* terrine; pâté

tête *f* head

T.G.V. *m* high-speed train

thé *m* tea; **thé au citron** lemon tea; **thé au lait** tea with milk; **thé nature** tea without milk

théière *f* teapot

thon *m* tuna(-fish)

ticket *m* ticket *(for bus, metro)*; **ticket de caisse** receipt; **ticket de quai** platform ticket; **ticket repas** meal voucher

tiède lukewarm

tiers *m* third party

tilleul *m* lime (tree); lime tea

timbale *f* pastry mould

timbrage *m* : **dispensé de timbrage** postage paid

timbre *m* stamp

tirage *m* printing; print *(photo)*; **tirage ce soir/le mercredi** lottery draw this evening/on Wednesdays

tirez pull

tisane *f* herbal tea

tissé(e) woven

tissu *m* material; fabric

tissu-éponge *m* terry towelling

titre *m* title; **à titre indicatif** for information only; **à titre provisoire** provisionally; **titre de transport** ticket

titulaire *m/f* holder of *(card etc)*

toboggan *m* flyover *(road)*; slide *(chute)*

toi you *(familiar form)*

toile *f* canvas

toilette *f* washing

toilettes *fpl* toilet; powder room

tomate *f* tomato; pastis with grenadine cordial

tomme (de Savoie) *f* mild soft cheese

ton your *(familiar form)*

tonalité *f* dial(ling) tone; **tonalité occupée** engaged signal

topinambour *m* Jerusalem artichoke

tordre to twist; **ne pas tordre** do not wring

torréfié(e) roasted *(coffee)*

tôt early

totalité *f* : **en totalité** entirely

toujours always; still

tour[1] *f* tower

tour[2] *m* trip; walk; ride; **tour de poitrine** bust measurements

touriste *m/f* tourist

touristique tourist

tournedos *m* thick slice of beef fillet; **tournedos Rossini** beef fillet with foie gras and truffles, in Madeira wine sauce

tourte *f* pie

tous all *(plural)*

Toussaint *f* : **la Toussaint** All Saints' Day

tout(e) all; everything; **tout droit** straight ahead; **toute la journée** all day

toutes all *(plural)*; **toutes directions**

through traffic

tout le monde everyone

toux *f* cough

train *m* train; **train autos-couchettes** car-sleeper train; **train à crémaillère** rack railway train

traiteur *m* caterer

trajet *m* journey

tranche *f* slice; **tranche napolitaine** block of Neapolitan ice cream

transférer to transfer

transfert *m* : **transfert libre** please organize your own transport (*to hotel etc*)

transpiration *f* perspiration

transport *m* : **transport d'enfants** children's bus; **transports en commun** public transport

travail *m* work

travaux *mpl* road works

travers de porc *m* pork spare rib

traversée *f* crossing (*voyage*)

très very; much

triangle *m* : **triangle de présignalisation** warning triangle

tricot *m* knitting; sweater; **tricots** knitwear

trimestre *m* term

tripes *fpl* tripe; **tripes à la mode de Caen** tripe cooked in cider and Calvados, with pig's trotters, vegetables and herbs

trois three

troisième third; **troisième âge** senior citizens; years of retirement

tronçon *m* section of road

trop too; **trop de** too much; too many

trottoir *m* pavement; **trottoir**

roulant moving walkway

trousse *f* case; kit; **trousse de pharmacie** first-aid kit; **trousse de toilette** toilet bag

trouver to find; **se trouver** to be (situated)

truffe *f* truffle

truite *f* trout; **truite aux amandes** trout cooked in butter and chopped almonds; **truite au bleu** boiled fresh trout

t.t.c. *see* taxe

tu you (*informal*)

T.V.A. *f* V.A.T.

ultérieur(e) later (*date etc*)

un(e) one; a; an

uni(e) plain (*not patterned*)

uniquement only

unitaire unit (*price*)

unité *f* unit

urgence *f* urgency; emergency; **d'urgence** urgently; **(service des) urgences** emergency unit

usage *m* use

usager *m* user

usine *f* factory

vacances *fpl* holiday(s); **en vacances** on holiday; **grandes vacances** summer holidays; **vacances scolaires** school holidays

vache *f* cow

vacherin *m* mild cow's-milk cheese; ice-cream in a meringue shell

vaisselle *f* crockery

valable valid

valider: validez votre ticket stamp/

punch your ticket

validité *f*: **durée de validité** (period of) validity; **validité illimitée** valid indefinitely

valise *f* suitcase

vannerie *f* wickerwork; basketwork

vapeur *f* steam

vaporisateur *m* spray *(container)*

varié(e) varied; various

V.D.Q.S. *see* **vin**

veau *m* calf; veal

végétal(e) vegetable

véhicule *m*: **véhicule de tourisme/ utilitaire** private/commercial vehicle

veiller: **veiller à ce que** (to) make sure that

vélo *m* bike

velouté *m*: **velouté de tomates** cream of tomato soup; **velouté de poireaux et pommes de terre** (cream of) leek and potato soup

venaison *f* venison

vendange(s) *f(pl)* harvest *(of grapes)*

vendeur *m* sales assistant

vendeuse *f* sales assistant

vendre to sell; **à vendre** for sale

vendredi *m* Friday; **le vendredi saint** Good Friday

venir to come

vente *f* sale; **en vente** on sale; **date limite de vente** sell-by date; **vente aux enchères** auction

verglacé(e): **chaussée verglacée** icy road surface

verglas *m* black ice

vérification *f* check(ing)

vérifier to audit; to check; **vérifiez**

la distance de visibilité keep a reasonable distance from car in front

verre *m* glass; **verres de contact** contact lenses

verrerie *f* glassware; glassworks

vers toward(s); about; **vers le haut** upward(s)

versement *m* payment; instalment

vert(e) green

verveine *f* verbena; verbena tea

veste *f* jacket

vestiaire *m* cloakroom

vêtements *mpl* clothes

vétérinaire *m/f* vet

veuillez: **veuillez consulter l'annuaire** please consult the directory

viande *f* meat; **viande séchée** thin slices of cured beef, usually eaten with pickles and rye bread *(Switz.)*

vichyssoise *f* cream of leek and potato soup

vidange *f* oil change *(car)*

vide empty

vie *f* life; **à vie** for life

vieille old

vieux old

vigne *f* vine; vineyard

vigueur *f*: **en vigueur** in force; current

ville *f* town

villégiature *f* holiday resort

vin *m* wine; **vin du cru** locally grown wine; **vin délimité de qualité supérieure (V.D.Q.S.)** classification for a quality wine, guaranteeing it comes from a particular area; **vin de pays** good but not top-class wine; **vin en pichet/bouteille** wine by the carafe/bottled wine

vinaigrette *f* vinaigrette sauce (oil, wine vinegar and seasoning); salad dressing

virage *m* bend *(in road)*; curve; corner; **virage sans visibilité** blind corner; **virage sur 2 km** bends for 2 km

visage *m* face

viser to stamp *(visa)*

visite *f* visit; consultation *(of doctor)*; **visite guidée** guided tour

visser to screw; **visser à fond** to screw home

vite quickly; fast

vitesse *f* gear *(of car)*; speed; **vitesse limitée à ...** speed limit ...

vitre *f* pane; window *(in car, train)*

vitrine *f* shop window

vivre to live

voeu *m* wish; **meilleurs voeux** best wishes

voici here is/are

voie *f* lane *(of road)*; line; track *(for trains)*; **par voie buccale/orale** orally; **voie de droite** inside lane; **voie express** expressway; **voie ferrée** railway; **voie de gauche** outside lane

voilà there is/are

voilier *m* yacht; sailing boat

voisin(e) *m/f* neighbour

voiture *f* car; coach *(of train)*

vol *m* flight; theft; **vol régulier** scheduled flight

volaille *f* poultry

voleur *m* thief

volonté *f* will; **à volonté** as much as you like *(wine etc)*; **des circonstances indépendantes de notre volonté** circumstances beyond our control

vos your *(polite, plural form)*

v.o.s.t. original version with subtitles *(film)*

votre your *(polite, plural form)*

vôtre: le/la vôtre yours

vous you; to you *(polite, plural form)*

Vouvray *m* dry, sweet and sparkling white wines from the Loire

voyage *m* journey; **voyage aller-retour** round trip; **voyage organisé** package holiday

voyageur *m* traveller

voyant *m* light

vrai(e) real; true

vue *f* view; sight; **vue imprenable** open outlook

wagon *m* carriage; waggon

wagon-couchettes *m* sleeping car

wagon-restaurant *m* dining car

wallon(e) of French-speaking Belgium

w-c *mpl* toilet; **w-c séparés** separate toilets

xérès *m* sherry

y there; on it; in it

yaourt *m* yoghurt

yeux *mpl* eyes

zone *f* zone; **zone piétonnière/piétonne** pedestrian precinct